Clear**Revise**®

BTEC Tech Award Level 1/2 in
Enterprise

Illustrated revision and practice

Component 3: Marketing and finance for enterprise

Published by
PG Online Limited
The Old Coach House
35 Main Road
Tolpuddle
Dorset
DT2 7EW
United Kingdom

sales@pgonline.co.uk
www.clearrevise.com
www.pgonline.co.uk
2022

PG ONLINE

PREFACE

Absolute clarity! That's the aim.

This is everything you need to ace the exam and beam with pride. Each topic is laid out in a beautifully illustrated format that is clear, approachable and as concise and simple as possible.

Each section of the specification is clearly indicated to help you cross-reference your revision. The checklist on the contents pages will help you keep track of what you have already worked through and what's left before the big day.

We have included worked exam-style questions with answers. There is also a set of exam-style questions at the end of each section for you to practise writing answers. You can check your answers against those given at the end of the book.

LEVELS OF LEARNING

Based on the degree to which you are able to truly understand a new topic, we recommend that you work in stages. Start by reading a short explanation of something, then try and recall what you've just read. This will have limited effect if you stop there but it aids the next stage. Question everything. Write down your own summary and then complete and mark a related exam-style question. Cover up the answers if necessary but learn from them once you've seen them. Lastly, teach someone else. Explain the topic in a way that they can understand. Have a go at the different practice questions – they offer an insight into how and where marks are awarded.

ACKNOWLEDGEMENTS

The questions in the ClearRevise textbook are the sole responsibility of the authors and have neither been provided nor approved by the examination board.

Every effort has been made to trace and acknowledge ownership of copyright. The publishers will be happy to make any future amendments with copyright owners that it has not been possible to contact. The publisher would like to thank the following companies and individuals who granted permission for the use of their images in this textbook.

Design and artwork: Jessica Webb / PG Online Ltd
Graphics / images: © Shutterstock
Indoor skydiving © naimtastik / Shutterstock

First edition 2022   10 9 8 7 6 5 4 3 2 1
A catalogue entry for this book is available from the British Library
ISBN: 978-1-910523-39-1
Contributor: Kelly Adams
Copyright © PG Online 2022
All rights reserved

Printed on FSC certified paper by Bell and Bain Ltd, Glasgow, UK.

THE SCIENCE OF REVISION

Illustrations and words

Research has shown that revising with words and pictures doubles the quality of responses by students.[1] This is known as 'dual-coding' because it provides two ways of fetching the information from our brain. The improvement in responses is particularly apparent in students when they are asked to apply their knowledge to different problems. Recall, application and judgement are all specifically and carefully assessed in public examination questions.

Retrieval of information

Retrieval practice encourages students to come up with answers to questions.[2] The closer the question is to one you might see in a real examination, the better. Also, the closer the environment in which a student revises is to the 'examination environment', the better. Students who had a test 2–7 days away did 30% better using retrieval practice than students who simply read, or repeatedly reread material. Students who were expected to teach the content to someone else after their revision period did better still.[3] What was found to be most interesting in other studies is that students using retrieval methods and testing for revision were also more resilient to the introduction of stress.[4]

Ebbinghaus' forgetting curve and spaced learning

Ebbinghaus' 140-year-old study examined the rate at which we forget things over time. The findings still hold true. However, the act of forgetting facts and techniques and relearning them is what cements them into the brain.[5] Spacing out revision is more effective than cramming – we know that, but students should also know that the space between revisiting material should vary depending on how far away the examination is. A cyclical approach is required. An examination 12 months away necessitates revisiting covered material about once a month. A test in 30 days should have topics revisited every 3 days – intervals of roughly a tenth of the time available.[6]

Summary

Students: the more tests and past questions you do, in an environment as close to examination conditions as possible, the better you are likely to perform on the day. If you prefer to listen to music while you revise, tunes without lyrics will be far less detrimental to your memory and retention. Silence is most effective.[5] If you choose to study with friends, choose carefully – effort is contagious.[7]

1. Mayer, R. E., & Anderson, R. B. (1991). Animations need narrations: An experimental test of dual-coding hypothesis. *Journal of Education Psychology*, (83)4, 484–490.

2. Roediger III, H. L., & Karpicke, J.D. (2006). Test-enhanced learning: Taking memory tests improves long-term retention. *Psychological Science*, 17(3), 249–255.

3. Nestojko, J., Bui, D., Kornell, N. & Bjork, E. (2014). Expecting to teach enhances learning and organisation of knowledge in free recall of text passages. *Memory and Cognition*, 42(7), 1038–1048.

4. Smith, A. M., Floerke, V. A., & Thomas, A. K. (2016) Retrieval practice protects memory against acute stress. *Science*, 354(6315), 1046–1048.

5. Perham, N., & Currie, H. (2014). Does listening to preferred music improve comprehension performance? *Applied Cognitive Psychology*, 28(2), 279–284.

6. Cepeda, N. J., Vul, E., Rohrer, D., Wixted, J. T. & Pashler, H. (2008). Spacing effects in learning a temporal ridgeline of optimal retention. *Psychological Science*, 19(11), 1095–1102.

7. Busch, B. & Watson, E. (2019), *The Science of Learning*, 1st ed. Routledge.

CONTENTS

Section C Financial planning and forecasting

MARK ALLOCATIONS

Green mark allocations[1] on answers to in-text questions throughout this guide help to indicate where marks are gained within the answers. A bracketed '1' e.g. [1] = one valid point worthy of a mark. There are often many more points to make than there are marks available so you have more opportunity to max out your answers than you may think.

Six mark questions require extended responses. These answers should be marked as a whole in accordance with the levels of response guidance on **page 75**.

COMMAND VERBS

The exam paper will use the following command verbs in each question.
Answering questions in the correct way can considerably increase your overall grade for the paper.
Study each of the command verbs below along with their meanings and how they are used to answer a question.

Give / State

Recall one or more pieces of information. These are short answers with 1 mark for each point.

Give **two** solutions to a cash flow problem.   [2]

Sell unused assets(1), gain investment(1), cut costs(1), delay payments(1), chase debtors(1), increase revenue(1).

Complete

Provide some missing information for a given table or diagram.

Complete the purchase order using the information given in Figure 1.   [1]

Item	Quantity	Price	Total
Butter	8 kg	£7 / kg	£56 (1)
Milk	20 l	0.50 / l	£10 (1)

Figure 1

Match

Match one option with another.

Match the following market segmentation methods by type.   [3]

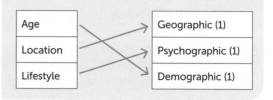

Age → Demographic (1)
Location → Geographic (1)
Lifestyle → Psychographic (1)

Explain

An explain question needs two parts. First give an example and then give a linked reason why this example answers the question. Make sure to use words such as 'because' or 'so' in this type of question.

Gibbs Bakery is concerned that its profit margins are too low.

Explain one way in which *Gibbs Bakery* could reduce its costs.   [2]

The bakery should find cheaper suppliers (1) ●--- *Example*
which would reduce the cost of raw materials (1). ●--- *Reason*

Label

Label information provided in a source material, for example, a diagram or table.

Study Figure 2. Label the break-even point. [1]

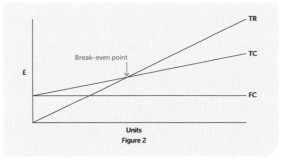

Figure 2

Draw

Produce a diagram, for example, a break-even chart.

The drawing should be labelled and annotated.

Using the information provided, draw and label the break-even chart. [4]

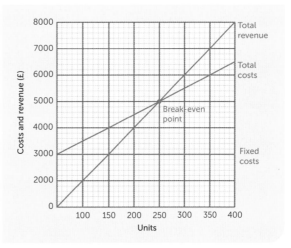

Discuss

Identify the problem or issue in the question.

Explore the relevant points that relate to the problem or issue with logical thoughts or arguments.

Think how they interrelate.

Links to content within either Component 1 or 2 will be expected in these questions.

You should use full paragraphs to answer these questions.

The full answer will usually be around a page of text.

Grants Buses are considering switching from cash to contactless card payments on board their vehicles.

Discuss the advantages and disadvantages of accepting electronic payments. [6]

Drivers will no longer need to deal with coins and change. This will mean they spend less time at stops and increase the punctuality of the service. Passengers without cash can use the service more easily, but those who do not have contactless payment technology may no longer be able to use the service. Turning away customers would not be popular and could reduce revenues. Those people relying on bus services most, may also be those who don't use payment cards.

Accurate and relevant knowledge

Detailed knowledge

Relevant to the question context

Clear links between points

Evaluate

1) Write down all the factors or events that apply to a given context.

2) Consider the strengths and weaknesses of each.

3) Identify those that are most important.

4) Give a reasoned conclusion supported by evidence.

Links to content within either Component 1 or 2 will be expected in these questions.

You should use full paragraphs to answer these questions.

The full answer will usually be around a page of text.

SureGym wants to promote a new 'Parent and child' morning.

They are considering marketing this on social media or printed flyers.

Evaluate which method would be best to increase interest and customers for the new event.   [6]

SureGym could make use of free advertising features in social media which would help keep marketing costs down. They could also set this up very quickly and measure the response. However, negative responses would be public and may deter other readers.

...

Printed flyers could be designed and printed in a few days. Someone would need to be employed to hand them out. Flyers could be kept and read at any time, but it is harder to measure the response.

...

In conclusion, young parents are likely to have a social media account and may be well suited to this approach. Social media offers a greater opportunity to reach people as they can also share the posts with their wider friendship groups. Whereas, flyers would be less immediate and more limited in their reach.

Accurate and relevant factor

Importance of the factor

Pros and cons

Alternative arguments

Conclusion is supported by evidence

Justification linked to question

Calculate

Find a numerical answer to a question. Show your working and include the units.

Study Figure 2. Calculate the Gross Profit Margin (GPM) for *Yarro Ltd*.   [1]

GPM = (GP ÷ Revenue) × 100

62 000 ÷ 112 000 × 100 = 55%

TOPICS FOR COMPONENT 3
Marketing and finance for enterprise

Information about the externally assessed exam

Written exam: 2 hours
60 marks
All questions are mandatory
40% of the qualification grade
Assessment type: External synoptic
Guided learning hours: 48

Specification coverage

Marketing activities, financial documents and statements, financial planning and forecasting.

The content for this assessment will be drawn from the essential subject content in sections A to C of Component 3 in the specification.

Questions

A mix of short answer and longer answer questions assessing knowledge, understanding and skills in contextual scenarios building on all components within the qualification.

TARGET MARKET

A **market** is any location where buyers and sellers come together to exchange money for goods or services. A **target market** is the likely customer group that an enterprise wants to sell its products (goods and services) to.

What is a typical target market?

A typical target market is usually a group of customers who exhibit similar characteristics. These can include age, location, income, or hobbies.

Enterprises usually try to identify who might buy their products before they stock or produce them so they can think about how much demand there might be or how to best advertise the goods or services they sell. Focused marketing messages are more effective and more likely to reach people who will make a purchase.

1. Alex wants to open a healthy snack bar opposite the local gym at a university in the city centre.

   Give **two** characteristics of a typical customer of the snack bar. [2]

   1. Two from: Interested in fitness,[1] healthy eating,[1] university students,[1] city workers,[1] dietary needs.[1]

The importance of establishing a target market

Knowing who the enterprise's likely customers are allows the business to develop a strong **brand**. A brand is an identifying feature that enterprises can use to distinguish their products from their competitors. This might consist of logos, symbols, or words. The brand can then be developed to attract the customers the enterprise is aiming the product at.

2. Jaheen is opening a new café. Jaheen has found two available locations. One is a second floor venue in the town centre. The other is on the ground floor of the local arts centre near a park. Jaheen has identified retirees as the primary target market.

   Explain **two** considerations for the most suitable location for Jaheen's enterprise. [4]

   2. Upstairs would be difficult for Jaheen's customers as it would limit access for anyone with mobility issues[1] which would impact potential footfall / sales.[1]

   Ground floor access may widen the target market to new parents and carers with prams[1] which would potentially increase revenue.[1]

   The arts centre and park is likely to attract a wide variety of customers[1] who may be inclined to stay at the café longer given a more relaxing environment than the town centre.[1]

   The town centre may have more people passing, and attract a younger audience[1] but they have less disposable income / don't fit the target market, which could reduce revenue / spend.[1]

A 'product' refers to a good or a service.

MARKET SEGMENTATION

Market segmentation can be used to make identifying a target market easier for an enterprise. This involves dividing a market into different groups called **market segments**.

Dividing customers into groups

Enterprises **segment** or divide the market according to demographic, geographic, psychographic and behavioural characteristics of potential or current customers. By doing this, they can match and market goods and services to suit the unique sets of needs of these groups. Segmentation also allows an enterprise to target advertising more effectively as it can focus on designing promotional material which appeals to the particular segments they target.

Knowing and understanding the target market also allows an enterprise to identify future areas of growth as it becomes more aware of the interests and needs of its target market. Meeting customer needs more effectively will allow an enterprise to improve its interactions with them. This will help to build brand loyalty, increasing its retention of customers.

The process of market segmentation involves splitting a larger market into smaller different groups. The main types of groups are demographic (e.g. age, race), geographic (location e.g. local, regional), psychographic (e.g. social class, lifestyle) and behavioural (e.g. spending, consumption). Enterprises can use one or more of these segments to identify and develop their target market.

Abby and Grace and live by the seaside. They want to set up a surfing shop in the local town.

Explain **two** advantages to an enterprise of segmenting the market. [2]

An enterprise might gain a competitive advantage[1] because targeting its products at the right people may increase sales.[1]

Segmentation identifies a target market[1] which allows an enterprise to concentrate its efforts in advertising products to the right consumers / to consumers' specific needs and wants.[1]

An enterprise can better satisfy the needs of a specific set of customers[1] if it can identify a common set of requirements that it can meet with its products.[1]

DEMOGRAPHICS

Demographic market segmentation is one of the easiest ways to segment a customer group. It allows an enterprise to market products (goods and services) to those with specific, common variables such as age, gender and education.

Advantages of demographic segmentation

Identifying a group with shared population characteristics helps an enterprise to build up a profile of what a typical customer might look like. This helps with decisions in marketing and purchasing as products can be targeted towards this type of customer.

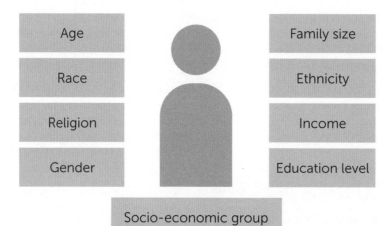

Age		Family size
Race		Ethnicity
Religion		Income
Gender		Education level

Socio-economic group

Age

Depending on a person's **age**, they may have different interests, tastes or needs. Often, enterprises use age to segment the market as different kinds of products will appeal to different age ranges. For example, children's toys will appeal to a younger age range.

Ethnicity

Ethnic groups share common attributes such as history or culture. These attributes can influence purchasing decisions. For example, paper lanterns are commonly associated with Chinese culture so could be targeted at people of Chinese origin at festival time.

Race

Some products can also be separated by **race**. Plasters and tights are commonly produced for varying skin tones.

Income

Income is a popular way of segmenting a market. Goods and services can be targeted at different income levels. People with higher incomes are more likely to buy luxury items.

Religion

Religion can influence customers choice of food, clothing and other items. For example, Muslim and Jewish people cannot eat pork meat. Vegetarianism is strongly linked with Buddhism and Hinduism.

Education level

Education increases knowledge and skills which, in turn, impact job opportunities and income. A better education of diet, for example, can lead to healthier lifestyle choices which can influence food and activity preferences.

Gender

Segmentation by **gender** is now seen as a contentious issue due to the different types of gender which exist. Traditionally, goods or services were divided into markets based on male or female genders according to their interests and needs. For example, aftershave is typically worn by males whereas perfume is worn by females. Additional forms of gender are also recognised which enterprises may target.

Family size

Products and services can also be segmented by **family size**. Larger families tend to incur greater household expenditure with increased amounts of food. Products can be tailored in size to meet the requirements of varying family sizes or individuals. Milk, crisps and tins, for example, are often sold in a range of volumes or in 'family size', 'share size', single and 'snack size' portions.

Socio economic group

Socio economic groups are based on a wide range of factors such as income, occupation and education. There are six groups A, B, C1, C2, D and E. Sometimes enterprises will wish to target a certain socio-economic group with a product based on their job roles or the likely income associated with those roles. Ties and shirts, for example, may be targeted at groups A to C1.

Social Grade	Description	Approximate % of UK population
A, B	Higher and intermediate managerial, administrative, professional occupations	22
C1	Supervisory, clerical and junior managerial, administrative, professional occupations	31
C2	Skilled manual occupations	21
D, E	Semi-skilled and unskilled manual occupations, Unemployed and lowest grade occupations	26

Explain **one** way in which using demographic segmentation can help an enterprise. [2]

Marketing is more efficient,[1] because the market is divided up into smaller segments to focus on.[1] The best way to reach customers is clearer,[1] because each segment will be based on / have similar customer characteristics.[1]

GEOGRAPHIC SEGMENTATION

Geographic segmentation helps an enterprise to target products or services at people who live in, travel to, or shop in a particular location.

Location

When using geographic segmentation, it is presumed that people in this location may have similar interests, wants and needs. In addition to location, geographic segmentation can be influenced by climate, culture, population and language.

Examples:

- An enterprise supplying outdoor swimming pools will target warmer areas or countries with their products.

- Restaurants and takeaways will customise menus according to local tastes and cultures. For example, pie, mash and liquor is a traditional East London meal often served with jellied eels.

- A clothing retailer near to a ski resort will stock clothing according to the temperature in the region.

- Retail outlets such as shopping centres will be more successful in densely populated areas where there is a greater number of potential customers.

- In areas with large international communities or tourists, enterprises may also offer information about their products translated into other languages.

Facebook advertising can target any user whose smartphone has been located in a particular area at a given time. Using this information, a seller of popular band t-shirts could target advertisements to anyone who has been within 500m of a stadium on the night they played.

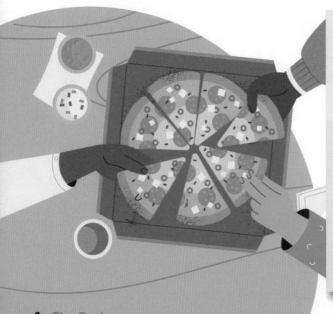

Gino runs a popular upmarket Italian restaurant and takeaway service for handmade pizzas. Pizzas are made using the finest organic ingredients and priced above those of other competitors locally.

Explain **two** ways that Gino could segment the market for the Italian restaurant. [4]

Gino's likely target market is very local[1] because they need to be able to receive a pizza while it is still hot.[1] Because the pizzas are handmade and more expensive, Gino should target wealthier customers[1] who can more easily afford the food.[1] Groups who lead busy lifestyles[1] may like the convenience of a delivery service, even for an additional cost, which could widen the delivery catchment / increase the size of the local market.[1]

PSYCHOGRAPHIC SEGMENTATION

Psychographic segmentation helps enterprises identify and group customers based on their attitudes, lifestyle choices, social class and personality characteristics.

Social media advertising can be targeted at anyone who has previously shown or declared an interest in specific areas.

Segments

People are rapidly segmenting themselves into smaller 'interest tribes' such as Ironman athletes, barbeque enthusiasts, Minecraft players, or environmental activists. Psychographic segmentation is therefore becoming more essential for enterprises in order for them to capitalise on rapidly changing attitudes and lifestyle choices.

Social class

Social class segmentation focuses on the social status of the customer. There are four types of social class: upper class, middle class, working class, lower class. Enterprises may target one of these groups to sell their products to. Poundland, Asda and Waitrose each target different groups.

Attitudes and values

Attitude segmentation targets customers based on a shared set of values. For example, some 'green' products are targeted at consumers who want to be environmentally friendly. Veganism has become popular, so enterprises target plant-based food products at this group.

Lifestyles

Lifestyle segmentation groups customers based on the type of lifestyle they live. This is influenced by their activities, interests, personalities and opinions. People may live active, healthy, bohemian, nomadic, solo or rural lifestyles, for example, or a combination of those. Products can be tailored to suit groups more closely.

Personality characteristics

Some enterprises choose to segment by **personality characteristics**. For example, supermarkets often have a quiet hour where no music is played, and lighting is toned down. This is designed to produce a calmer shopping environment for those who may prefer this.

Amy wants to find out about trends in the food industry before opening a small food store in the local shopping centre.

Explain **one** advantage to an enterprise of researching current trends. [2]

An understanding of current trends will help determine what an enterprise should sell / help define its target market,[1] which will increase its chance of success / increase revenue.[1]

BEHAVIOURAL SEGMENTATION

Behavioural segmentation distinguishes potential and current customers in terms of their shopping behaviour. This includes how much they spend, how much they consume, how often they use something, if they are loyal to brands and how they perceive desired benefits.

Spending

An enterprise can analyse **customer spend** patterns to identify shopping trends and preferences. This can inform enterprises of the popularity or need for premium or value ranges, which can then influence their advertising towards the relevant groups. Spending patterns can be affected by the economy, costs of living and levels of unemployment.

Consumption

When deciding on what products or product sizes to sell, enterprises may look at **consumption** to help segment the market. Consumption is how much of something customers are using or purchasing. This is often influenced by the time of year, holidays, the weather and promotions. For example, a 2-for-1 offer on BBQ food on a hot bank holiday weekend will increase sales.

Usage rate

Usage rate is usually combined with consumption and examines how often customers are buying a product. This can help with advertising and stock ordering. Many people change their cars every three years so showrooms may choose to target advertising of a new model after 2½ years.

Loyalty status

Brand loyalty focuses on repeat customers, their needs and their shopping patterns. On the other hand, it can identify those who have never made a purchase. It measures the level of loyalty a customer has towards a brand either through what they buy or how they interact with the enterprise. Enterprises can monitor brand loyalty through store loyalty cards, special offers or incentives such as a frequent flyer program. Doing this allows them to identify stock needs and advertise more effectively to the right people.
Examples include frequent flyer miles and supermarket points cards.

Desired benefits

Many products have features that provide benefits to the customers purchasing them. For example, people may buy super-fast broadband as they think this will give them better internet speeds. **Benefit segmentation** targets these customers based on desired benefit needs.

MARKETS

Enterprises sell to **consumers** or to other **businesses**. Some will do both. The market an enterprise operates in will define its target customers.

Business to Business (B2B)

An enterprise operating in a **business to business (B2B)** market only sells its goods to other enterprises. For example, a potato farmer may sell his potatoes to a wholesaler, manufacturer or restaurant who will make potato products such as chips with them.

B2B markets tend to consist of larger enterprises as these types of organisations are more likely to sell in bulk and use more expensive ways of advertising such as face to face selling. These enterprises are also quite efficient and are able to supply a large amount of stock quickly.

Business to Consumer (B2C)

A **business to consumer (B2C)** enterprise sells its goods to individual customers, for example, a portion of chips from a fish and chip shop. B2C markets target consumers by using a wide variety of advertising methods such as social media, radio, online advertising, email and discount codes.

Brand perception is important in a B2C market due to the level of competition faced by enterprises. Given the size of the whole market, a clearly defined segment or target market is also important.

Mass markets and niche markets

Whether an enterprise operates in a B2B market or a B2C market, it will need to decide if it will be targeting the masses or just a small segment of people.

A plumber's merchant may sell products to trade and to the general public. This would make them both B2B and B2C.

Mass markets

A **mass market** approach requires the promotion of goods or services to a wide variety of audiences, trying to appeal to as many people as possible. An example of a company operating in the mass market is *Apple Inc*.

Comcare is a charity shop selling used items and clothing directly to the consumer.

    (a) Give the name of this type of market. [1]

    (b) Explain whether they are targeting a mass or niche market.   [2]

(a) B2C. [1]

(b) Comcare is targeting a mass market [1] *because they are aiming their products at all / most sectors of the market / as many people as possible.* [1]

Niche markets

A **niche market** approach focuses on targeting a smaller segment of a larger market; a specific target audience who have specialised needs and wants. For example, *Lefty's* is an online website selling items designed for left-handed people.

SCENARIO

Simon Anderson operates in the B2B market running *EasyBuild Furniture Supplies*, which specialises in manufacturing low-cost furniture for big office spaces.

The enterprise has recently experienced severe competition from enterprises who can sell similar products more cheaply. Simon has decided that the enterprise may need to move away from the B2B market and focus on those customers who can provide higher profit margins. Simon has decided to investigate the B2C market as a potential option.

Simon has noticed that there has been a noticeable trend towards working from home and homeowners are increasingly converting spare rooms into offices. Simon has no experience of dealing with customers directly. Simon needs to identify who is most likely to buy the furniture and if it is worth moving into the B2C market.

Simon has two options:
- Continue trading in the B2B market
- Move into the B2C market.

Evaluate which of the two options would be best to ensure the continued profitability of the enterprise. [6]

Example answer

Advantages of continuing in the B2B market
- *Simon knows the market well. They are already an established supplier / there might be a possibility they could manufacture products more cheaply using alternative materials.*
- *The enterprise has previously been very profitable / it could try to find a cheaper supplier or accept a lower profit margin in exchange for larger orders.*
- *EasyBuild already has a relationship with customers and may have brand loyalty.*

Disadvantages of continuing in the B2B market
- *Competitors in the B2B market may price Simon out of the market which could causes losses. It may no longer be profitable enough to continue.*
- *More people are moving out of offices indicating that the market space is in decline.*

Advantages of moving to the B2C market
- *Potentially large customer base.*
- *Increase in people working from home means there is more demand for office furniture.*

Disadvantages of moving to the B2C market
- *Very little opportunity to sell in bulk.*
- *Marketing may cost more / need a different approach which will take time to learn.*
- *The B2C market may require different styles of furniture which may need a lot of design and development investment before production can begin.*

The conclusion should recommend either the B2B or B2C market with justifications from the analysis to support the conclusion. The use of context is important to support the conclusion.

Long answers must be written in paragraphs. Bullet points have been used here to make the answers easier to understand. This type of question will be marked using a Levels Based Marks Scheme. See page 75 for details.

EXAMINATION PRACTICE

(a) Give **one** reason why *Pineham Indoor Sky Diving* would be considered to be operating in a niche market. [1]

Pineham Indoor Sky Diving is considering opening additional venues in Edinburgh and Cardiff. They are considering using geographical segmentation as part of their research.

(b) Give **two** other ways *Pineham Indoor Sky Diving* could segment their current market. [2]

(c) Explain **one** advantage to an enterprise of segmenting the market. [2]

(d) Explain **one** advantage to *Pineham Indoor Sky Diving* of using geographical segmentation for their expansion projects. [2]

Pineham Indoor Sky Diving is interested to find out more about their customers' usage rate.

(e) Explain **one** method an enterprise could use to do this. [2]

Pineham Indoor Sky Diving are considering offering additional experience packages to enterprises.

(f) Discuss the advantages and disadvantages to *Pineham Indoor Sky Diving* of trading in the B2B market. [6]

Pineham Indoor Sky Diving wants to attract more customers from the surrounding area.
It has decided to choose between two options:

- Offering premium experience packages to people in higher socio-economic groups.
- Target the local university to attract students living in student accommodation nearby.

(g) Evaluate which option would be best to attract more customers from the surrounding area. [6]

4Ps OF THE MARKETING MIX

The four Ps of marketing are more commonly known as the **marketing mix**. These are **product**, **price**, **place** and **promotion**. These factors describe the basic marketing decisions which an enterprise must make to produce a successful marketing strategy.

The mix

Each of the **4Ps** influences complements the others. For example, if an enterprise advertises (**promotion**) in the wrong **place** it will not matter so much how good the **product** is because the target market is unlikely to see it. The mix will change over time.

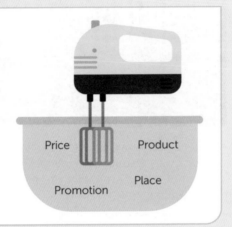

Price

Product

Promotion

Place

Matching marketing campaigns to the aims of an enterprise

An enterprise must consider its aims when applying the 4Ps. Any marketing campaign is going to cost money, so it is important that it helps achieve those aims. For example, if a taxi enterprise is trying to increase awareness of a new discounted fare for loyal customers in order to increase profit, it must ensure that any marketing strategies stimulate a response from this specific target market. Otherwise, the campaign may be unsuccessful, and a waste of time and funds.

Traditional and digital marketing methods

Traditional methods

These can include methods such as television and radio advertising, billboards, flyers, newspapers, magazines and catalogues.

Digital methods

These can include social media, pop up adverts, email, SMS, notifications from apps and influencer marketing.

Some methods will be more appropriate than others when working with the 4Ps to devise a marketing strategy. Often, a combination of different methods is used by enterprises to reach a wider audience.

A decision about which method to use often depends on the product being marketed and the target market. If the target market is more likely to engage with web-based technologies such as social media, then this may influence the decision to be made. Similarly, some groups are more likely to read newspapers, for example, so this may be a good strategy if an enterprise is targeting this segment.

Danny owns a specialist grocery store in a Manchester city suburb. Danny would like to increase the number of customers from the local community as they have started to supply a large range of new foods which have been requested by some of the local community through their social media page.

1. Give **two** methods Danny might use to advertise to this target market. [2]
2. Explain **one** reason why successful marketing might help Danny's enterprise achieve its goals. [2]

1. *Danny could use social media[1] or local radio.[1]*
2. *Manchester is a busy city, and his potential target market might listen to the radio during their commute. This might persuade them to visit Danny's shop.[1]*

   Attracting more customers will create more revenue[1] / may increase profit.[1]

PRODUCT

The **product** might be considered the most important element of the marketing mix. Without a good product that satisfies customer needs, the locations it is sold, its price and its promotion will not matter because consumers may not be interested in it.

Product portfolio

Enterprises may have a **product portfolio**. This comprises all of the products and services an enterprise offers. A product portfolio offers a wider spread of income so if one product is not doing so well, other products or services may increase to make up the revenue.

USP

It is important that a product has a **USP (Unique Selling Point)**. A USP is a feature of a product or service which separates it from competitors by, for example, its design or taste. By having a USP, a product can attract customers by distinguishing itself in the market.

Branding

Branding is particularly important in marketing a product. For a product to have the best chance of success, it is important the enterprise has a good **brand image**. Brand image is a customer's perception of an enterprise and its products. For example, many associate high quality, design and innovation with Apple. These feelings make up the **brand's personality**. A brand personality is a set of human characteristics attributed to a brand. Apple's slogan *"Think different"* echoes its personality.

Many enterprises have launched products which have not been successful such as *Google Glass* or *Clear Cola*. Undertaking market research before any decisions on products are made will reduce the risk of failure.

Explain **two** disadvantages to an enterprise of extending its product portfolio. [4]

More product lines will require more stock to be kept[1] which will cost more to buy / tie up more cash reserves in inventory / could decrease their liquidity ratio.[1]

A shop with greater product lines may need to share the existing shelf / advertising space between all of them[1] so an increase in products can decrease the space for each.[1]

Employees may need to be trained to demonstrate / deal with technical enquiries into new products[1] which may cost the enterprise additional time and money.[1]

New products pose a risk / may not be profitable if not properly researched[1] and could damage business reputation[1] / reduce profitability.[1]

THE PRODUCT LIFE CYCLE

Enterprises use the **product life cycle** to evaluate product life span. The product life cycle is a method that describes a product's stages from its introduction to the market until it is removed from the market. There are five stages: **development**, **introduction**, **growth**, **maturity**, and **decline**.

The phases of the product life cycle

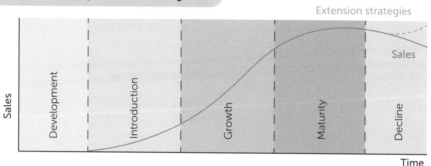

Development	Introduction	Growth	Maturity	Decline
Research and development is employed to come up with a marketable product. As this is pre-launch, no sales are made, but the enterprise incurs many costs, so related cash-flow is negative.	The product is launched onto the market. Sales start to increase. Cash-flow is likely to remain negative as the enterprise must heavily promote the product to develop awareness of it.	Sales will start to rise more rapidly after a successful launch as customers become more familiar with the product. As sales start to rise, cash-flow starts to become positive.	Sales levels and cash-flow are at their highest. However, growth in sales will start to slow down. The market may become saturated as more competitors enter the market.	Sales of the product decrease. This may be because the product is outdated. If this continues, the enterprise may decide to withdraw the product.

! Note

Different products can be at different stages of this product life cycle at different times. Not all products reach the decline stage. Consider Coca-Cola. This product continues to be at the maturity stage despite being released over 100 years ago.

Extension strategies

Sometimes a product can saturate the market and stop increasing in sales. To try to increase sales of this product, an enterprise might use a product extension strategy. For example, Coca-Cola introduced Diet Coke in 1982 to extend this product.

Brenda sells burgers on a food truck. Brenda has noticed that the truck's new homemade vegan burger has become much more popular over the last few months.

Identify the likely position of the vegan burger on the product life cycle. [1]

Growth stage. [1]

PRICE

Price is the value that is placed on the good or service offered. When marketing a product, it is important to set the correct price.

Pricing strategies

Many factors affect price depending on the product, its quality, the method of promotion the enterprise wishes to use and what the competitors are charging. Based on these factors an enterprise can use various different pricing strategies. A **pricing strategy** is a way of setting a price so that the enterprise can achieve its marketing aims and objectives.

Price penetration

Price penetration sets a lower price when a product is introduced to the market which increases as the product becomes more established. This helps the product or service to enter the market and gather an existing customer base who hopefully remain loyal to the brand.

Price skimming

Price skimming sets a high initial price, usually because the product might be highly desired or of superior quality to competing products. As the product or service ages, the price lowers to try to continually attract new customers. Games console manufacturers often use this strategy.

Competitive pricing

Competitive pricing means that enterprises set their prices based on those of their competitors. They either try to undercut them or to at least match their prices.

Premium pricing

Premium pricing involves pricing products above the competition to try to establish a perception of quality and that of a luxury brand.

Cost plus

Cost plus is a calculation that identifies how much a product will cost to produce and adds a percentage markup onto this for profit.

Mankish has recently opened a Turkish barber in a busy city high street.

(a) A barber cut costs Mankish £8 to deliver the service. Calculate the price they should charge using the cost plus method and a 30% markup. [1]

(b) Explain **one** disadvantage of using competitive pricing for Mankish. [2]

(a) 8 × 1.3 = £10.40.[1]

(b) Mankish is less well established than the competition[1] and low initial prices may not cover the start up and running costs.[1] Competitive pricing assumes others have set the right price[1] but they may be in financial trouble and matching their errors may be a mistake.[1] / Competitive pricing only really works if your good or service has better features than the competition.[1]

PLACE

Place considers the location where products can be found and how they are distributed from the manufacturer to the end user.

Physical and digital distribution

Products need to be positioned in a location where the target market will see them and hopefully purchase them.

Place can either be a physical location, for example, a shop where customers can visit to purchase a good or service, or it can be virtual. **E-commerce** describes internet retail (buying and selling). This could be through a website or an app on a phone or games console. The distribution of outlets across an area will affect sales. Some manufacturers will use a retailer to sell their products on their behalf. Others may consider direct distribution via their own stores or, more commonly, their own website.

Enterprises often use both of these methods as a way to increase exposure to their target audience and to create additional ways for customers to view, test, purchase or return products.

Jasmine and Gary own a high street retro game shop. They sell both video games and board games. They have noticed that fewer people are visiting the store area, and this is affecting their revenue. They are considering investing in a website for both 'bricks' and 'clicks'.

Explain **one** advantage to Jasmine and Gary of having a virtual store as well as a physical store. [2]

They will be able to reach more of their target market[1] which may increase sales for Jasmine and Gary.[1]

People who do not go to / live near the store can access[1] and buy products / can make purchases.[1]

An ecommerce site may increase brand awareness and exposure for the game shop[1] which may attract more customers.[1]

A virtual store can be open 24/7[1] which may increase sales after the high street shop has closed.[1]

Some enterprises work together to increase sales for them both. Bookstores with internal coffee shops have been popular in recent years.

PROMOTION

Promotion is any activity which creates an awareness of an enterprise and its products. How an enterprise achieves this through a variety of promotional activities the enterprise engages in is called the **promotional mix**.

Promotional mix

Advertising involves persuading or informing customers about products or enterprises, their features and benefits and how the customer can make a purchase. Common advertising methods include television, billboards, radio, cinema, newspaper, and magazine advertising.

PR or **OPR** means (online) **public relations**. PR or OPR usually focuses on maintaining a positive image for an enterprise through press releases, building relationships with local communities or even engaging influencers.
- ➕ Can improve reputation
- ➖ PR could be negative

Social media marketing involves using different social media platforms to market an enterprise's goods or services. This could be in the form of a social network page or paid advertising. Posts could be in written form, short blogs or image orientated advertisements.
- ➕ Viral posts can quickly reach huge audiences
- ➖ Ads can be expensive and time-consuming

Direct marketing is a way of promoting a product directly to its target audience without mass media support from other enterprises. Common methods include direct mail or email, social media, phone calls, or text messages.
- ➕ Can build positive relationships with customers
- ➖ Can be ignored or unwanted as 'junk mail'

Personal selling involves using salespeople to talk to potential customers. A salesperson must have good selling skills to effectively generate sales.
- ➕ Can use telephone, video calls, email or face to face meetings
- ➖ Salespeople need to be fully trained and can be expensive to employ

Sales promotion can also be used to promote the enterprise's products and services. It is usually a short-term method to try to boost sales. These can be methods such as money off coupons, free gifts, offers, competitions, loyalty cards and point of sale materials.
- ➕ Can attract new customers or boost sales
- ➖ Discount offers or free gifts can reduce revenue and increase costs

OFFER!

If you read this coupon, so might real customers!

Coupons, competitions, loyalty incentives and discount offers can attract attention and increase sales.

QR codes (or Quick Response codes) promote interaction and engagement with the reader to provide more details.

Scan me!

ABOVE THE LINE AND BELOW THE LINE PROMOTION

The type of promotion used can fall into two categories: **above the line** or **below the line** promotion.

Above the line

Above the line methods use a mass media approach, such as television, for products that have a broad appeal, for example Dairy Milk.

Below the line

Below the line promotion methods are not mass media approaches. These are usually less expensive and more focused than above the line strategies. An enterprise must decide which method it wants to use in line with its marketing aims and objectives.

Radio advertising	TV advertising
Newspapers	Cinema
Billboards	Magazines
Direct mail	Sales promotion
Catalogues	Personal selling
Trade shows	Social media marketing

The line

MULTICHANNEL MARKETING

Multichannel marketing is a marketing approach that uses a variety of traditional and digital methods to communicate with customers.

The advantages of using multi-channel marketing is that an enterprise is more likely to reach a larger target market through different methods. It may also mean the target market will see the marketing more often, and in more places, strengthening their relationship and brand loyalty.

Multi-channel marketing campaigns must link to an enterprise's aims and objectives, in particular to their marketing objectives as these will dictate the main things that an enterprise wants to achieve. For example, profit, increased sales or an increase in customers using the enterprise.

Mears Smith is a garden centre on the outskirts of a town offering guided tours around their new show-garden with qualified salespeople.

A local newspaper has offered to write a story on their tour experience.

(a) Give **one** advantage of using public relations in this way. [1]

(b) Give **one** advantage of personal selling. [1]

(a) *It is usually free.[1] The story will be impartial and likely to have stronger appeal.[1] The message can be distributed to a wide audience.[1]*

(b) *The salesperson can adapt their own messages to suit individual needs.[1] Customers can ask questions to satisfy any unknowns or concerns.[1]*

SCENARIO

Fantasy Land is a fancy dress shop based on the outskirts of a town, with premium costumes for sale and collection-only hire. The market is quite competitive with several new fancy dress shops opening up in the last few years giving customers more choice over where they shop.

Fantasy Land is run by Orla McDonald and specialises in fantasy related costume. The superheroes and villains ranges are the best sellers, especially with parents purchasing costumes for children's parties.

The enterprise has responded to the competition by using competitive pricing to try to retain customers.

Fantasy Land is also considering how it can continue to be a viable enterprise.
It has two decisions to consider:

- To extend their product offer with a fancy dress hire mailing service around the UK.
- To change the enterprise location to the city centre where there is a higher footfall.

1. Explain **one** advantage to *Fantasy Land* of using competitor pricing for its products. [2]
2. Explain **one** disadvantage to *Fantasy Land* of offering a mail order hire service for its outfits. [2]
3. Explain **one** risk to *Fantasy Land* of relocating to the city centre to sell its products. [2]

Orla has decided that to expand the business, focusing on the fantasy products the enterprise has for hire or sale.

They are considering arranging a fashion show in the local shopping centre to showcase these items. Orla needs to attract her target market's parents to the event in order to generate potential sales.

They have decided on two potential methods of advertising the event:

- They will ask local enterprises to put posters of the event in their shop windows.
- They will use social media to promote the event.

4. Evaluate which of these two methods would be best for Orla to use to attract the parents of their target market to the fashion show. [6]

Example answers

1. *By using competitor pricing, Orla will be able to better persuade current customers to switch from a competitor[1] because Fantasy Land offers the same value for money.[1]*

2. *One disadvantage to Orla using a mail order service is that they increase their costs[1] as they would need to package, send and track the items.[1] There is no guarantee people who hire the costumes will return them in perfect condition[1] which may affect their ability to make profit.[1]*

3. *Relocation to the city centre is likely to incur higher rent[1] which means Orla will need to make more sales to break even.[1]*

4. **Advantages of asking enterprises to display their posters:**
   - Very little cost as the enterprise could produce these themselves.
   - Going to be distributed locally so potential customers are more likely to see them as they use the city centre.
   - Will be easy to read and stand out.
   - Can make them very visually appealing and showcase the best that Orla has to offer.

   Disadvantages of asking enterprises to display her posters:
   - Local enterprises may not be willing to display the posters as this detracts from their own enterprise.
   - They may want payment for this or a favour from Orla in return.
   - It may look unprofessional or tacky and spoil their brand image.
   - There will still incur printing costs and it will take time to visit each enterprise and ask for permission.
   - If any changes need to be made, all the posters will need to be reprinted.

   Advantages of posting on social media:
   - Can connect with a large amount of people.
   - Low cost.
   - Can easily and quickly post, it won't take Orla much time to do and it's easy to update.
   - Will attract attention easily and increase awareness of Jane's event and brand.

   Disadvantages of posting on social media:
   - Although people may see the posts, they may not attend the fashion show.
   - People may not live locally so it will not appeal to them.
   - Negative feedback on social media can hurt the brand / project's success.
   - The advertising will easily be seen by their competitors who could launch their own fashion show in a different location.

   A suitable conclusion is required for 'evaluate' questions. This may involve multichannel marketing using both methods. Refer to the guidance on 'evaluate' questions on page viii and the levels of response mark scheme on page 75.

FACTORS INFLUENCING THE CHOICE OF MARKETING METHODS

When deciding upon various marketing methods, an enterprise may first consider these five factors. Most enterprises will select just a few methods.

Appropriateness for product and brand image

Any marketing an enterprise does should reflect their **brand image**. This is particularly important when trying to attract the right target market. For example, a luxury brand may be more likely to promote themselves in high-end magazines than tabloid newspapers to remain associated with a premium lifestyle and to better fit the potential target audience. A luxury brand may devalue themselves by advertising in lower status publications or by using cheaper marketing methods. Their affluent target market may be unimpressed by any attempts to 'lower the clientele' as they like the status of being able to afford to shop there.

Speed and accessibility of information / ease of reaching target market

An enterprise must consider the **speed** at which it needs to reach its **target market** and how easy it is to provide the promotional information effectively. This will influence the promotional method it chooses and explains why many larger enterprises often use social media as a promotional tool for damage control as it is quick and provides an easy way to reach the target market.

Cost to the enterprise

Enterprises with little funds may choose more below the line promotion as they can narrow the target market and lower the **cost** by specifically targeting one area. This may, however, be less effective. Enterprises with more money might wish to engage in more above the line activities as this allows them to reach a larger potential audience and therefore more potential customers.

Competitors' activities

Enterprises should monitor their **competitors**. If a competitor is spending heavily on promotion, an enterprise must carefully consider its options as there is a risk this promotion will divert customers from their own enterprise. A likely response would be for the enterprise to respond to maintain parity with the competitor. For example, there are frequent price wars between the major supermarkets or between petrol companies.

Experience of the entrepreneur

An entrepreneur may have strong **knowledge** of their market and understand the needs of their customers well. Time and **experience** also builds reputation and encourages word of mouth. This means they may not need to promote their enterprise as much as a new competitor. A good local decorator, for example, may have such strong customer loyalty, they never need to advertise at all.

TRUST, REPUTATION AND LOYALTY

Importance of brand image

Building a strong **brand image** can attract and retain customers for an enterprise. Brand image is a customer's perception of a product or enterprise. It conveys what they can expect from the enterprise in terms of **quality**, **variety**, and **customer service**. Consider Poundland and Boots. Both brands convey different messages in terms of quality and value to consumers and are therefore more likely to attract different target markets.

! Note

When marketing, an enterprise must consider the brand image it wants to convey and how this will fit in with the identified target market.

In 2013, leading supermarkets were found to be selling products containing horsemeat instead of 100% beef as expected. This damaged reputation as customers were unhappy about being mislead.

Importance of reputation

Reputation is everything when attracting new customers and trying to retain old ones. The actions of an enterprise can very much affect public opinion. To improve reputation, enterprises may engage in different kinds of practice to attempt to gain customers.

Being environmentally friendly: Enterprises might adopt environmentally friendly practices such as reducing plastic and using recycled materials. This shows **social responsibility** as they are taking responsibility for their own actions. Doing this is known to appeal to some segments of the market.

Improving customer service: Good **customer service** has a positive impact on brand image, e.g. John Lewis, as it elevates status as a trustworthy enterprise. Poor customer service devalues brand image as it leads to complaints and a lack of trust.

Rejecting unethical practice: Enterprises may reject **unethical** or **controversial marketing strategies**. Using them might otherwise alter consumer perception of the brand. Using children to promote fast food can be considered unethical and may cause some customers to stop using a brand.

Helping the community: Many enterprises try to improve their reputation by getting involved in local community events, either through **sponsorship**, **donations** or **prizes**. In return, the brand can be seen to support the area in which the target market live. This should boost brand image as customers are more likely to buy from enterprises who they have a social connection with.

Jasmine runs a coffee shop and offers one free cup for every ten purchased.

Explain **one** advantage to Jasmine of using a loyalty incentive to promote sales. [2]

Loyalty cards provide an opportunity to increase sales[1] by enticing customers to make repeat purchases.[1] Customers choose your enterprise over your competitor's[1] because they receive a reward / feel more valued.[1] Customers may feel more comfortable / spend longer in the shop[1] which can encourage additional sales, e.g. pastries, from Jasmine.[1]

Raheem owns *Pizza Delight*, a fast-food enterprise based in Sheffield city centre operating for 20 years. During this time, *Pizza Delight* has built up a small but loyal customer base of mainly students and office workers. The enterprise employs two full time workers, Jo and Adam. Jo deals with telephone orders and complaint resolution. Adam deals with food production and service. All their packaging for the food is made from recycled packaging in line with the brand's environmental principles.

Raheem is considering expanding the enterprise to include a food truck in the same name. Raheem is thinking of placing this in an area near two secondary schools.

The local community are unhappy with this. To overcome this, Raheem is thinking of introducing some healthier options to the menu as well as giving talks in the school about the benefit of healthy eating. They hope by doing this they will be able to negate any effect on their reputation.

1. Explain **one** impact on *Pizza Delight*'s brand image as a result of using recyclable packaging. [2]
2. Explain **one** disadvantage to the reputation of a food truck enterprise opening near a school. [2]
3. Explain **two** possible effects on the enterprise's reputation as a result of a focus on healthy eating. [4]

Jo has been nominated for a customer service award in the local newspaper.
4. Explain **one** impact this could have on the enterprise's reputation. [2]

Adam has recently found a dough supplier which costs the same as Raheem's current supplier but delivers better quality products.
5. Explain **one** way this might affect *Pizza Delight*'s brand image. [2]

Raheem has decided they should promote their new food truck. They have decided on two options:
- To advertise via a flyer, handed out to the people who work in the area.
- To advertise on the local radio station during off peak hours.

6. Evaluate which of these **two** methods would be best for Raheem to use to attract their target audience.

   You must consider:
   - Speed and accessibility of reaching the target market
   - The cost to the enterprise
   - The appropriateness of the product and its brand image

   You must also develop a reasoned conclusion identifying which would be the best option for Raheem. [6]

Example answers

1. Pizza Delight's brand image might improve[1] because by using recyclable packaging, people will know the enterprise cares about the environment.[1]

2. A food truck opening near a school may negatively affect the reputation of the enterprise because parents and teachers care about the welfare of students[1] and will be worried they will purchase food that could make them unhealthy and overweight.[1]

3. Adding healthier options to the menu might have a positive impact on their reputation because the local community will feel cared for[1] with a new range of products especially for their benefit.[1] By educating local school children, the enterprise is giving something back to the community[1] which may help inform students so in future they eat more healthily.[1] The community may see this positively as the enterprise is educating students[1] even though it might reduce their sales[1] and take them away from their core business.

4. People will hear about the good customer service and nomination which puts the enterprise in a positive light[1] meaning more people might try their products.[1]

5. The enterprise's brand image may improve because it will be able to offer better quality products for the same price.[1] This means that Raheem's products will be seen as being better value than before.[1]

6. *Advantages of choosing flyers*
   - Generally low cost, quick and easy to print and use.
   - Can quickly hand out to local people who are likely to be in their target market.
   - Can tailor them for the target market with an appropriate message.
   - Could align well with the brand image of a small independent enterprise.

   Disadvantages of choosing flyers
   - People may not read them or put them straight in the bin.
   - Difficult to know how many they will need.
   - The reputation of the enterprise may be affected if there are any spelling errors or the presentation is poor.
   - May become expensive depending on the print quality and number required.

   Advantages of advertising on the local radio off peak
   - Cost effective to produce.
   - Everyone who listens to the radio at that time will hear the advert at the forefront of the broadcast.
   - Can target all listeners to the radio station in the local area, who might drive to their venue.
   - Can produce effective, catchy and memorable adverts.

   Disadvantages of advertising on the local radio off peak
   - An off-peak slot means fewer listeners will hear it.
   - As it is mass media, they may hit listeners who would not be interested in their products.
   - A radio advert can take time to plan, record and test.
   - It is quite an expensive method to use, however, it will be cheaper off peak than on peak.

A reasoned conclusion is required for 'evaluate' questions. Refer to the guidance on page viii and the levels of response mark scheme on page 75.

EXAMINATION PRACTICE

> **Scenario: *Papillon Artisan Bakery***
>
> Zara has successfully run Papillon, an artisan bakery stall, for five years. They make speciality ethnic and traditional breads, offering a variety of high-quality baked goods.
>
>
>
> Zara's stall is in a local indoor market, and has a steady, loyal customer base. They usually advertise via social media and also sometimes in the local newsletter produced by the community centre. They offer a special ten percent discount to regular customers via a loyalty card.
>
> To set up the enterprise Zara segmented the market.

(a) Give the name of this promotion strategy. [1]

After two months, Zara decides they are going to concentrate on using below the line promotion.

(b) Zara uses posters and sales discounts. Give **two** other examples of below the line promotion. [2]

(c) Explain **two** advantages of using below the line promotion to promote an enterprise. [4]

Zara has decided to grow the stall online by creating a website. They will also add to their product portfolio by adding a filled sandwich range. Zara is trying to decide which methods of promotion to use to promote to this new target market. They have a budget of £500 to spend on promotion.

There are **two** factors that will influence Zara's choice of promotion.

- The new target market
- A budget of £500

(d) Explain how each of these two factors may influence the promotional methods chosen:
  (i) The new target market. [2]
  (ii) A budget of £500. [2]

(e) Explain **one** benefit to Zara of adding to their product portfolio. [2]

Zara has been asked by the local community centre to sponsor an event.

(f) Explain **one** reputational benefit to an enterprise of sponsoring a local event. [2]

(g) Zara uses a premium pricing strategy.
  (i) Explain what is meant by a premium pricing strategy. [2]
  (ii) Give **one** disadvantage of using this strategy. [1]

FINANCIAL DOCUMENTS

All enterprises need to complete and interpret **financial documents**. This is so they can keep an accurate and detailed record of the transactions they participate in. This will help an enterprise to identify its financial position and accounting obligations at any time.

Purchase order

The purpose of a **purchase order** is to record an order from the buyer to the supplier. These are usually completed on a form which lists the goods or services that will be purchased from the enterprise.

Below is an example of a completed purchase order form. Once completed, the purchase order will be sent to the enterprise, to start the buying and selling process.

> **! Note**
>
> The sequence of financial documents for B2B enterprises usually follows that shown on the next few pages of this guide. B2C enterprises often prefer to invoice before goods and services are provided.

The customer completes the purchase order form and sends it to the supplier

Delivery address

The date of ordering is entered, and a unique purchase order number created for reference

Name and address of supplier

Unique purchase order number for reference.

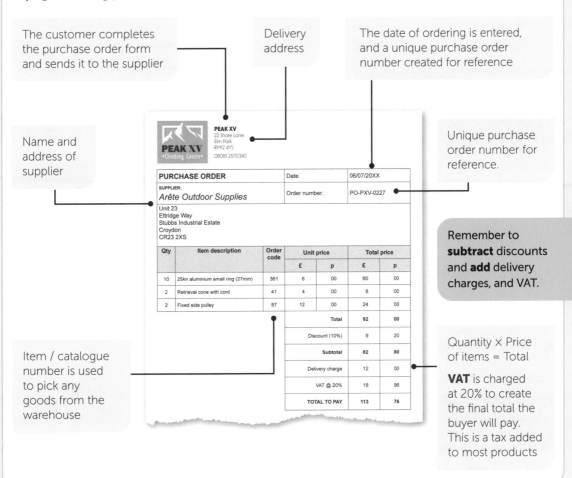

Item / catalogue number is used to pick any goods from the warehouse

Remember to **subtract** discounts and **add** delivery charges, and VAT.

Quantity × Price of items = Total

VAT is charged at 20% to create the final total the buyer will pay. This is a tax added to most products

---

PEAK XV
22 Shore Lane
Elm Park
RM12 4YS
0808l 2570340

PURCHASE ORDER	Date:	06/07/20XX
SUPPLIER: *Arête Outdoor Supplies*	Order number:	PO-PXV-0227

Unit 23
Ettridge Way
Stubbs Industrial Estate
Croydon
CR23 2XS

Qty	Item description	Order code	Unit price £	Unit price p	Total price £	Total price p
10	25kn aluminium small ring (27mm)	361	6	00	60	00
2	Retrieval cone with cord	41	4	00	8	00
2	Fixed side pulley	87	12	00	24	00
			Total		92	00
			Discount (10%)		9	20
			Subtotal		82	80
			Delivery charge		12	00
			VAT @ 20%		18	96
			TOTAL TO PAY		113	76

DELIVERY NOTE

A delivery note is a document which is sent by the supplier with the ordered goods. It repeats the quantity of goods ordered and lists them. Customers can use a delivery note to check the goods ordered match the goods sent.

The customer may be required to sign to say the information on the delivery note matches what has been sent. If this is not correct, then this should be logged on a **goods received note**.

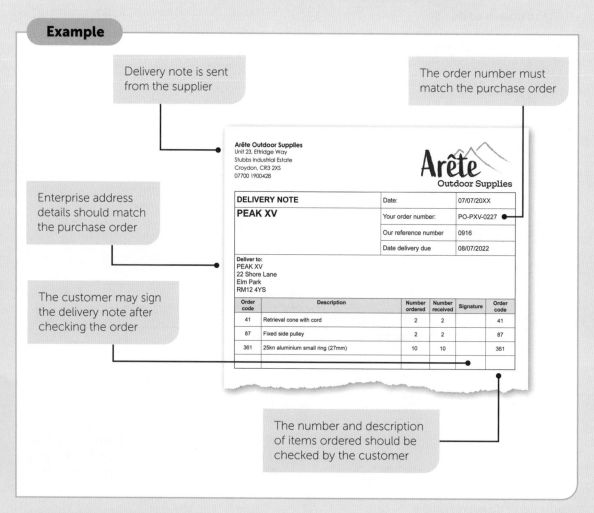

Example

Delivery note is sent from the supplier

The order number must match the purchase order

Enterprise address details should match the purchase order

The customer may sign the delivery note after checking the order

The number and description of items ordered should be checked by the customer

1. Give **two** features of a delivery note. [2]
2. Explain **one** reason why it is important for the delivery note to have a reference number. [2]

1. *Item number,[1] Qty,[1] Delivery date,[1] Order number,[1] Supplier name, [1] Customer details.[1]*
2. *If there are any problems with the order then the reference number will help locate the original purchase order[1] so the issue can be investigated and resolved.[1]*

GOODS RECEIVED NOTE (GRN)

A **goods received note**, or **GRN**, is a document which shows what goods were actually received. It is commonly used internally within the purchasing enterprise, often by warehousing staff, especially where delivery notes do not require a signature.

A GRN provides a record of what has been received and should be checked against what was originally ordered. If any discrepancies are found, they should be logged on the form for the supplier to action.

Once goods have been received, a supplier will send out an **invoice** for payment.

Example

PEAK XV
22 Shore Lane
Elm Park
RM12 4YS
08081 2570340

GOODS RECEIVED NOTE (GRN)		Date:		08/07/20XX
FROM: *Arête Outdoor Supplies*		GRN number:		00-0334

Unit 23
Ettridge Way
Stubbs Industrial Estate
Croydon
CR3 2XS

Qty	Item description	Order code	Condition of goods
2	Retrieval cone with cord	41	
2	Fixed side pulley	87	
10	25kn aluminium small ring (27mm)	361	Missing 2 rings

The warehouse may sign below to say an order has been received and checked

Goods should be checked and any problems noted for action by the supplier

Explain what should happen if the products received are damaged or do not match the original purchase order. [2]

The supplier should be notified [1] who may authorise the return/replacement/additional delivery of goods to match the original order.[1]

INVOICE

An **invoice** is issued as a request for payment. Its purpose is to provide a formal statement to show what a customer has bought and to provide them with payment details.

Any refunds may be issued separately, so in this case, the shortfall of two aluminium rings will still be invoiced for and refunded using a **credit note**.

The invoice should have the correct invoice and delivery address

The invoice date determines which tax year the invoice falls into for both enterprise's accounts

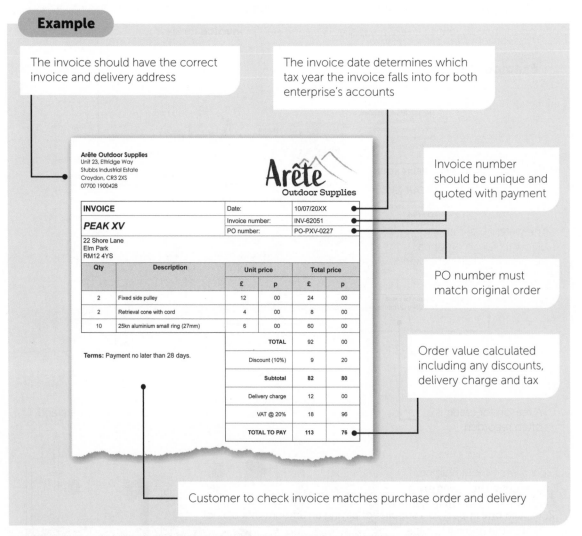

Invoice number should be unique and quoted with payment

PO number must match original order

Order value calculated including any discounts, delivery charge and tax

Customer to check invoice matches purchase order and delivery

1. Explain **one** impact to the buyer of making a late payment. [2]
2. Explain **one** impact to the supplier of receiving a late payment. [2]

   1. *The reputation of the buyer may suffer with the supplier[1] who may choose not to supply them or offer further credit.[1]*
   2. *The supplier may have cash flow issues[1] as they were expecting funds sooner.[1]*

It is unlikely that you will need to calculate a discount percentage, delivery charge and VAT for the same task.

CREDIT NOTE

A **credit note** notifies a customer of a reduction in the amount they are due to pay as a result of a missing, incorrect or damaged order. Its purpose is to credit the customer for any difference in value with their original or intended order.

Example

The supplier will usually specify a processing time for the refund or credit

Unique credit note number for reference

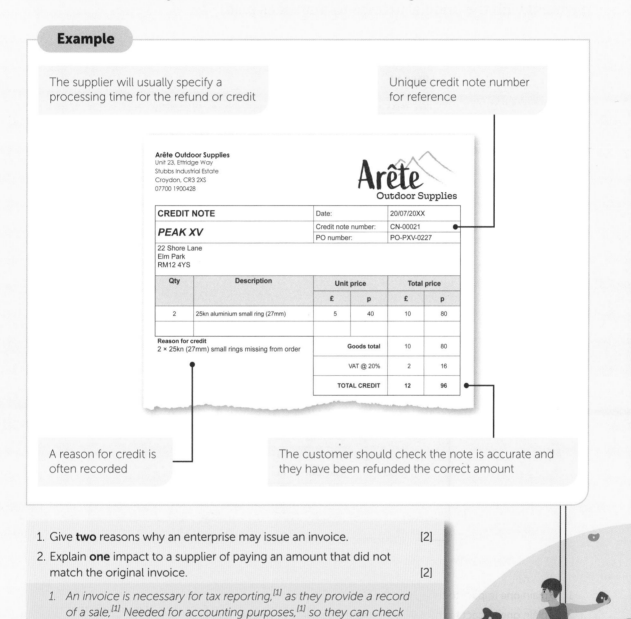

Arête Outdoor Supplies
Unit 23, Ettridge Way
Stubbs Industrial Estate
Croydon, CR3 2XS
07700 1900428

Arête
Outdoor Supplies

CREDIT NOTE			Date:		20/07/20XX	
PEAK XV			Credit note number:		CN-00021	
			PO number:		PO-PXV-0227	

22 Shore Lane
Elm Park
RM12 4YS

Qty	Description	Unit price		Total price	
		£	p	£	p
2	25kn aluminium small ring (27mm)	5	40	10	80

Reason for credit 2 × 25kn (27mm) small rings missing from order	Goods total	10	80
	VAT @ 20%	2	16
	TOTAL CREDIT	12	96

A reason for credit is often recorded

The customer should check the note is accurate and they have been refunded the correct amount

1. Give **two** reasons why an enterprise may issue an invoice. [2]
2. Explain **one** impact to a supplier of paying an amount that did not match the original invoice. [2]

1. *An invoice is necessary for tax reporting,[1] as they provide a record of a sale.[1] Needed for accounting purposes,[1] so they can check against any bank payments received.[1]*

2. *The supplier may not be able to match up the paid amount to the correct invoice[1] so may need to go back to the buyer to ask for more details.[1] A credit note or additional request for payment would be required[1] which would need further time to create or resolve.[1]*

REMITTANCE ADVICE

A **remittance advice slip** accompanies any payment to let the supplier know that an invoice has been paid. Its purpose is to provide proof of payment from the customer to the supplier and to help the supplier to match the bank payment with the original invoice to mark it as paid.

The total amount should match the amount owing on the invoice

A customer reference or invoice number is crucial to help the supplier match up the payment correctly

RECEIPT

A **sales receipt** is a document that proves a payment has been made and received. It provides a detailed record of a transaction between a buyer and a seller.

Transaction date

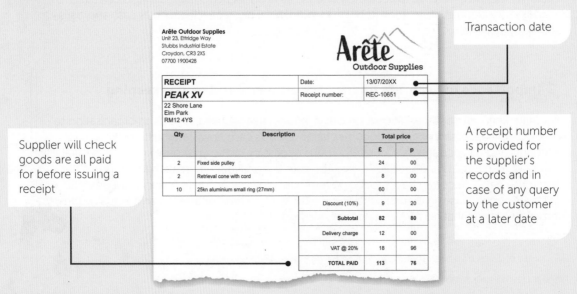

Supplier will check goods are all paid for before issuing a receipt

A receipt number is provided for the supplier's records and in case of any query by the customer at a later date

STATEMENT OF ACCOUNT

A **statement of account (SOA)** shows all the transactions that have taken place between a buyer and seller. Its purpose is to detail any transactions between both parties, to itemise payments made and clearly indicate any outstanding balance.

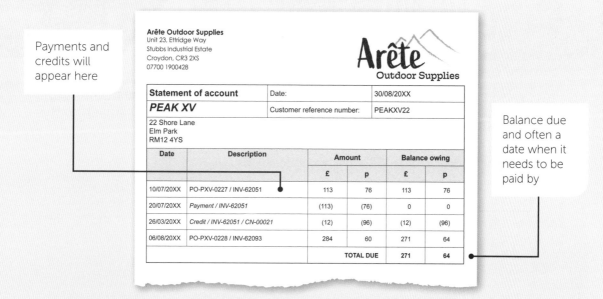

Payments and credits will appear here

Balance due and often a date when it needs to be paid by

Arête Outdoor Supplies
Unit 23, Ettridge Way
Stubbs Industrial Estate
Croydon, CR3 2XS
07700 1900428

Arête
Outdoor Supplies

Statement of account	Date:		30/08/20XX	
PEAK XV	Customer reference number:		PEAKXV22	
22 Shore Lane Elm Park RM12 4YS				

Date	Description	Amount		Balance owing	
		£	p	£	p
10/07/20XX	PO-PXV-0227 / INV-62051	113	76	113	76
20/07/20XX	Payment / INV-62051	(113)	(76)	0	0
26/03/20XX	Credit / INV-62051 / CN-00021	(12)	(96)	(12)	(96)
06/08/20XX	PO-PXV-0228 / INV-62093	284	60	271	64
			TOTAL DUE	271	64

Importance of accuracy when documents are being used

It is vital for enterprises to record all information on these documents accurately. This is because, at any time, an enterprise needs to know what they have paid out and what they are owed by debtors. This will help the enterprise to accurately analyse its financial performance and to calculate its accounts. Inaccurate information could lead to financial discrepancies such as cash shortfalls and overpayments.

Importance of accurate financial documents and record keeping

Accurate financial documentation is crucial to business accounting. It helps an organisation to produce any necessary financial documentation such as cash flow statements, profit and loss accounts and balance sheets accurately. This is necessary so the enterprise knows its profitability and how many assets and liabilities it has. Accurate financial documentation also ensures the enterprise pays the correct taxes to the government. Without accurate financial documents, mistakes might cause an enterprise to assume it has more cash or assets than it actually does. It may also mean that tax / VAT is under or overpaid.

Mike owns *Links DIY* in the centre of a town. *Links DIY* sells a wide variety of DIY materials including paint, gardening supplies and power tools. Mike offers goods at a competitive price compared to high street chains and is used by many local trades people.

They are preparing an invoice for a local painter and decorator for supplies.

1. (a)   Complete the invoice using the information provided. [5]

LINKSDIY

Links DIY | 18 High Street | Frome | BA11 8KW | 07700 9001229

INVOICE		Date:		31/03/20XX	
Merritt Painting & Decorating		Invoice number:		466	
		PO number		PO-MPD-014	

37 Peter's Close
Westbury
BA13 4YJX

Qty	Description	Unit price		Total price	
		£	p	£	p
100	Paintbrush	8	00	800	00
10	Turpentine (1 Litre)	3	50	(i)	
50	Lining wallpaper (Roll)	5	50	(ii)	
		TOTAL		1110	00
Terms: Payment within 30 days		Delivery charge		**30**	**00**
		Subtotal		(iii)	
		VAT @ 20%		(iv)	
		TOTAL TO PAY		(v)	

Remember to show the pence to two decimal places.

(b)   Describe **one** reason why it is important for Mike to keep an accurate record of this purchase. [2]

(c)   Mike discovers an error has been made on the invoice. The customer ordered 10 paintbrushes and not 100.

Explain **one** impact of this error on Links DIY. [2]

2. Mike has asked you to complete a credit note for the refund against the paintbrushes. Complete the credit note using the information in Question 1. [6]

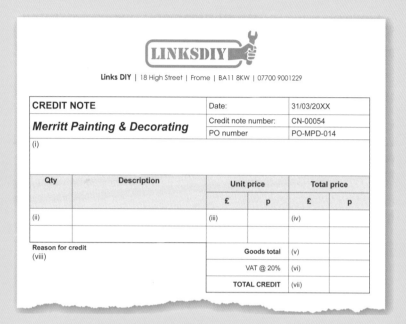

LINKSDIY

Links DIY | 18 High Street | Frome | BA11 8KW | 07700 9001229

CREDIT NOTE		Date:	31/03/20XX
Merritt Painting & Decorating		Credit note number:	CN-00054
		PO number	PO-MPD-014
(i)			

Qty	Description	Unit price		Total price	
		£	p	£	p
(ii)		(iii)		(iv)	

Reason for credit (viii)		Goods total	(v)	
		VAT @ 20%	(vi)	
		TOTAL CREDIT	(vii)	

Example answers

1. (a) In descending order down the column – (i) £35.00, (ii) £275.00, (iii) £1140.00, (iv) £228.00, (v) £1368.00.[5]

    (b) It is important for Mike to keep an accurate record of the purchase so the accounts are accurate[1] which will help the enterprise with its end of year accounts / tax calculations.[1] In the event of a dispute with the purchaser[1] the records of sale can be checked to find if / where an error may have occurred for resolution.[1]

    (c) Overcharging customers / delivery errors may affect the supplier's reputation[1] because customers may lose trust in the enterprise and will be worried in future that they might make errors again, so may go to a competitor.[1] Invoicing errors will also affect the enterprise's accounts / stock control which will no longer be accurate[1] creating incorrect historical records to check back on.[1] The invoice may need to be reissued / a credit note will need to be issued[1] which will delay the payment / incur additional cost in time and administration.[1]

2. Six from: (i) Address for Merritt Painting and Decorating, (ii) 90 Paintbrushes (iii) 8.00 (iv) 720.00 (v) 720.00 (vi) 144.00 (vii) 864.00, (viii) Quantity error.[6]

PAYMENT METHODS

There are lots of ways an enterprise can make and receive payments for goods or services. The choice of method is usually down to the customer; however, it can be restricted by enterprises in terms of what payments they will accept.

Convenience

Some payment methods are more suitable than others depending on the transaction being made. For example, at a busy football stadium or fast food restaurant, contactless payment is preferred so that customers can be served quickly. The more methods an enterprise can offer, the more convenient it is for customers and the more it may fit with their lifestyles.

Payment methods and their impact on customers

Cash

Cash is commonly carried in wallets for small purchases.

- ⊕ Cash is accepted by most enterprises and is a quick form of payment.
- ⊕ Cash can only be accepted in a face-to-face transaction and cannot be used online.
- ⊖ Stolen cash is difficult to trace so it is not usually used for big transactions.
- ⊖ Mistakes can be made counting change.

Credit cards and debit cards

The difference between a **credit card** and a **debit card** is that a debit card payment comes directly from the customers bank account; whereas on a credit card the payment comes from the customer's credit card provider and is loaned to the customer. They will have to pay it back later. With a debit card, a customer will be limited by the available balance in their account, or the transaction will be declined. With a credit card, the customer will have a credit card limit that they can spend up to before repaying some of the money borrowed on the card.

- ⊕ Both credit and debit cards can be used in many locations.
- ⊕ They both offer chip and pin, and contactless payments.
- ⊕ They can also be used over the phone and online.
- ⊕ Loyalty points or cashback can be offered on purchases.
- ⊕ Credit cards can postpone payments which can help with budgeting and personal cash flow.
- ⊖ Lenders that issue credit cards charge interest on the balance owed by the card holder. Both cards carry a small transaction fee for the enterprise.
- ⊖ Cards can be lost, stolen or cloned.
- ⊖ Credit card funds will need to be paid back at some point and can lead to mounting debt for some people.

> Fraudulent card payments are inconvenient for the customer as accounts are frozen while new cards are reissued, but banks will often refund these once investigated.

Direct debits

Direct debit is a form of payment commonly used for large or regular purchases. It is an instruction to a bank authorising an enterprise to transfer money from a customer's account to the enterprise's account as payments for goods or services on a given date.

- ⊕ This is a simple way to pay regular bills, for example, utility bills.
- ⊕ Discounts are sometimes offered for paying by direct debit.
- ⊖ Transactions will be declined if the customer does not have sufficient funds in their account to cover the value of the debit instruction on the day it is due.
- ⊖ The amount taken for each payment can vary.

Payment technologies

Payment technologies are constantly evolving with new ways to pay for goods and services. This is a simple way to pay regular bills, for example, utility bills.

Apps such as **PayPal** and **Apple Pay** now allow quick and convenient payment directly from a mobile phone or watch. Contactless payments from a debit or credit card use similar technology to make payment without entering a PIN.

- ⊕ No need to carry bank cards or cash.
- ⊖ Can be limits on the value of the payment.

Impact on customers of using different payment methods

The use of technology opens up more potential spending choices. However, with all these, security and safety concerns emerge. It is becoming more common that cards can be cloned or stolen. Contactless payments do not require a PIN which creates a risk for the customer if their card is stolen. Similarly, a customer could have their card details hacked into via the internet or their bank log in details stolen. Whilst the increase of payment methods is good for enterprises, it does come with some risks to customers.

Impact on enterprises of using different payment methods

In order to maximise sales of products despite some of their drawbacks, it is important for an enterprise to offer a variety of payment methods in order to attract customers.

The following is a **summary of impacts** on an enterprise:

Cash – Requires a cash safe, a float for change and additional security to reduce the risk of theft, which increases the cost of use. Employees may also need training in handling cash.

Credit and debit cards – Need to purchase a reader and pay transaction processing fees. Fraudulent transactions can incur chargeback fees. Staff need to be trained to accepts card payments which increases wage costs for the training time.

Direct debit – An easy and secure way to collect flexible, regular payments, but the customer may cancel or not be able to pay.

Payment technologies – Need to rent the right equipment and pay for a mobile telephone network connection which can be costly. Malfunctions may prevent sales until fixed.

EXAMINATION PRACTICE

Scenario: *Franco Spares Ltd*

Frankie runs *Franco Spares Ltd*, a local enterprise specialising in bicycle parts and accessories. Frankie has many customers but prefers to accept cash as the enterprise gets the funds immediately. The enterprise also accepts card payments over the phone.

Frankie is now considering options on what to do next. Frankie is considering other payment options alongside creating a website for the enterprise as a lot of time is spent on the phone handling orders. Staff then need to create the right financial documents and despatch the orders.

1. Frankie recently received a trade credit order over the phone from the *Forest MTB Club*. The invoice for the order has now been paid.

   Frankie will need to prepare a receipt for their payment.
   • Disc brake pads are £9.99 each.
   • Inner tubes are £1.59 each.

Franco Spares Ltd
18 Lowes Close
Grinton, AN8 9XR
07700 9001331

FRANCO Spares Ltd

RECEIPT	Date:	13 Nov 20XX
Franco Spares Ltd	Receipt number:	06714

Forest MTB Club
Unit 5 Green Lane
Grinton
AN10 5YU

Qty	Description	Total price £	p
4	Bicycle cleaning fluid (5 Litre)	11	96
34	Disc Brake Pads (Pair)	339	66
67	26" × 1.75-2.1 Inner tubes (Schrader valve)	106	53
	Subtotal	458	15
	VAT @ 20%	91	63
	TOTAL PAID	549	78

   (a) Complete the receipt below. [5]
   (b) Give **one** appropriate method of payment for telephone orders. debit card [1]
   (c) Explain **one** reason why it is important for Frankie to provide a receipt. [2]
   proves a payment has been made/recieved
   important for tax records

2. Frankie has created a diagram to show the order of financial documents between themselves and the *Forest MTB Club*.

(a) Complete the diagram using the following document types. [3]
- Payment
- Purchase order
- Statement of account

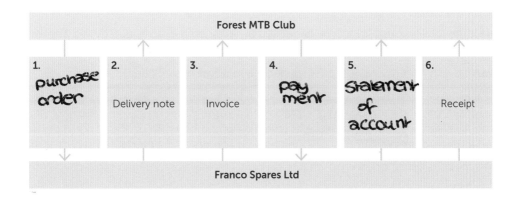

Forest MTB Club

| 1. purchase order | 2. Delivery note | 3. Invoice | 4. payment | 5. statement of account | 6. Receipt |

Franco Spares Ltd

(b) An extract from the statement of account for *Forest MTB Club* is shown below.

Date	Description	Amount		Balance owing	
		£	p	£	p
19 Sep 20XX	Invoice #3864	82	97	82	97
5 Oct 20XX	Payment	82	97	-	-
22 Oct 20XX	Invoice #3972	1110	40	1110	40
24 Oct 20XX	Payment	840	00	270	40
12 Nov 20XX	Invoice #3984	549	75	820	15
13 Nov 20XX	Payment	549	75	270	40

(i) Give the total amount owed by *Forest MTB Club* at the end of September. [1]

(ii) Give the total value of payments in October by *Forest MTB Club*. [1]

(c) Explain **one** advantage to *Franco Spares* of sending a statement of account to its customers. [2]

indicates any outstanding balance

3. Frankie prefers to take cash payments in the shop.

(a) Explain **one** disadvantage of accepting cash. [2]

Frankie is considering changing to accept more contactless payments using debit cards, credit cards or mobile phone payments.

(b) Explain **two** advantages of accepting contactless payments. [2]

REVENUES AND COSTS

Enterprises receive income from selling goods and services. In carrying out all of the operations of the enterprise, costs will also be incurred.

Revenue / turnover

Revenue is the total amount of income generated by an enterprise from its activities. The revenue of an enterprise can be calculated by the formula: **Revenue = Sales × Price Per Item**.

Turnover can also refer to revenue, but includes the turnover of stock and staff.

Revenue can come from many sources. It can come from cash and credit sales of goods, renting, or selling assets, offering a repair service, or receiving a commission on sales if operating for a third party. An enterprise should maximise its revenue opportunities. To do this, it could develop new product lines, offer sales promotions, find new customers or, if a product or service is in high demand, raise selling prices.

Costs

Start-up costs

Start-up costs are those that an enterprise needs to pay in order to start trading. These may depend on the type of enterprise being set up. Common examples of start-up costs include shop fittings, tools, machinery, vehicles, website construction, logo design and company registration fees.

Running costs

Running costs are those that an enterprise needs to pay as it trades day to day. These costs will vary according to how much the enterprise is making or selling and how much it costs to remain open. Common examples of running costs are stock, ingredients, website maintenance, utility bills and consumables.

An enterprise should minimise costs. Costs can affect the amount of **profit** an enterprise makes as these must be subtracted from the revenue. Lowering costs will give an enterprise a better chance of making profit. To lower costs, an enterprise could find cheaper suppliers, negotiate discounts with existing ones, consider its staffing arrangements or streamline its operations.

Finlay is a licenced trader selling fresh fish from a refrigerated van at a market stall.

1. Identify **one** start-up cost that Finlay is likely to have incurred. [2]

2. Give **two** running costs that Finlay is likely to incur. [2]

3. Finlay would like to know how much revenue he has made at the weekend.

   Finlay sold 40 cod loins at £9 each and 30 whole trout at £11 each.

   Calculate Finlay's revenue for the weekend. [2]

   1. One from: Vehicle,[1] trader's licence,[1] market stall.[1] Accept other valid costs.

   2. Two from: Fuel,[1] ice,[1] fish (stock),[1] bags/packaging.[1] Accept other valid costs.

   3. 40 × 9 = £360 + 30 × 11 = £330 £360 + £330 = £690 revenue. [2] One mark for correct workings.

PROFIT AND LOSS ACCOUNT

A **profit and loss account (statement of comprehensive income)** is a financial statement which shows the profit or loss of an enterprise over time, usually over a period of one year. It helps an enterprise to see how profitable it is.

Components of a profit and loss account

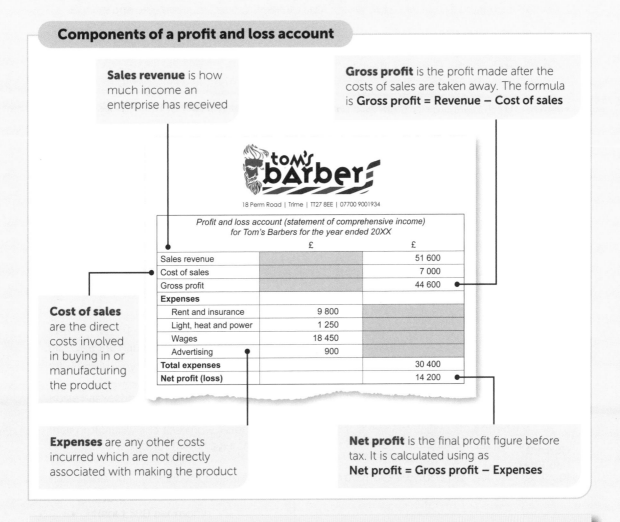

Sales revenue is how much income an enterprise has received

Gross profit is the profit made after the costs of sales are taken away. The formula is **Gross profit = Revenue − Cost of sales**

Cost of sales are the direct costs involved in buying in or manufacturing the product

Expenses are any other costs incurred which are not directly associated with making the product

Net profit is the final profit figure before tax. It is calculated using as **Net profit = Gross profit − Expenses**

18 Perm Road | Trime | TT27 8EE | 07700 9001934

Profit and loss account (statement of comprehensive income) for Tom's Barbers for the year ended 20XX

	£	£
Sales revenue		51 600
Cost of sales		7 000
Gross profit		44 600
Expenses		
Rent and insurance	9 800	
Light, heat and power	1 250	
Wages	18 450	
Advertising	900	
Total expenses		30 400
Net profit (loss)		14 200

Explain **one** way in which *Tom's Barbers* could increase its net profit next year. [2]

Look at ways to increase sales revenue[1] for example, offer promotions / price increases which are not going to put off customers / extended trading hours.[1]

Decrease the cost of sales by using cheaper suppliers / negotiating lower prices[1] which would increase gross profit[1] and therefore increases net profit.

Decrease expenses[1] by using cheaper suppliers / evaluating staffing needs/wages.[1]

BALANCE SHEET

A **balance sheet** (statement of financial position) is a financial statement that shows a snapshot of an enterprise's assets and liabilities at a point in time.

It is typically produced on the last day of the financial tax year. It helps an enterprise to see the value of its assets and how much it owes in liabilities. It also allows the enterprise to see how it finances its activities.

Components of a balance sheet

Fixed assets. These are the long-term assets of an enterprise

Total assets. This is the value of the assets of an enterprise when fixed and current assets are added together

Current assets. These are owned by the enterprise and expected to be used or sold in the next year

Current liabilities. These are debts that the enterprise must pay within 1 year

Total assets less Current liabilities. The owner's equity or share capital plus profits

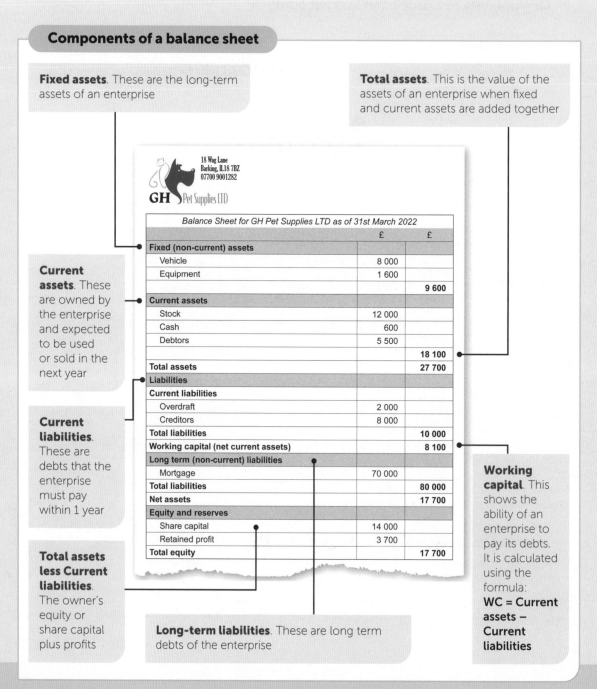

18 Wag Lane
Barking, IL18 7BZ
07700 9001282

GH Pet Supplies LTD

Balance Sheet for GH Pet Supplies LTD as of 31st March 2022		
	£	£
Fixed (non-current) assets		
Vehicle	8 000	
Equipment	1 600	
		9 600
Current assets		
Stock	12 000	
Cash	600	
Debtors	5 500	
		18 100
Total assets		27 700
Liabilities		
Current liabilities		
Overdraft	2 000	
Creditors	8 000	
Total liabilities		10 000
Working capital (net current assets)		8 100
Long term (non-current) liabilities		
Mortgage	70 000	
Total liabilities		80 000
Net assets		17 700
Equity and reserves		
Share capital	14 000	
Retained profit	3 700	
Total equity		17 700

Working capital. This shows the ability of an enterprise to pay its debts. It is calculated using the formula:
WC = Current assets − Current liabilities

Long-term liabilities. These are long term debts of the enterprise

Assets and liabilities

Asset

An **asset** is something of value owned by an enterprise.

Current assets can change, and include cash, debtors and stock

Fixed assets include vehicles, equipment and buildings. These are the longer-term assets of an enterprise.

Liability

A **liability** is a debt owed by an enterprise.

Current liabilities include payments that are commonly due within a short term period. These include creditors, loan and overdraft repayments.

Long-term liabilities are long-term debts, such as a mortgage.

Remember: Debtors (accounts receivable) owe an enterprise money. Creditors (accounts payable) are owed money by an enterprise.

The value of equity is calculated as the difference between assets and liabilities on an enterprise's balance sheet. It represents the value of the owner's investment.

Capital

Capital is money that is available to an enterprise. A start-up capital fund may help get an enterprise running. It will aim to increase its capital reserves through **retained profit**, in order to invest in future projects.

STAKEHOLDERS

A **stakeholder** is a party or person who has an interest in the enterprise and its activities. Stakeholders will be interested in the financial health of the enterprise, as indicated in the financial statements.

Owners

Enterprise **owners** will be keen to know if their enterprise is making a profit and how easily they are able to pay any debts. The financial statements allow an owner to check profitability and liquidity, and, if necessary, to take steps to preserve the financial health of the enterprise. For example, selling off assets to reduce liabilities.

Managers

Managers will want to know if the enterprise has met its targets for revenue or cost savings, and what profit (loss) has been achieved. Managers may then adjust elements of enterprise operations. Their pay may also be linked to performance based on these figures.

Lenders

Lenders include banks, investors and other enterprises offering credit terms. Their funds are invested into an enterprise and are at stake should it fail. Loans or credit are only likely to be provided if the enterprise can prove it is able to pay them back.

Employees

Employees will want to know that an enterprise is operating well for their own job security.

Suppliers

Suppliers will want to know an enterprise can pay any credit they have been given. They will also have an interest because they may want to continue trading with the enterprise.

Government

Tax authorities will want to make sure that accounts are accurate, and that the enterprise is paying the right amount of tax. Limited companies are required to submit their annual accounts to the government.

Customers

Customers will be interested in the financial health of the enterprise as they will want to know that any goods they have paid for will be sent. They also want to ensure that an enterprise will survive to honour any guarantees offered.

QNB is a camping supplies store. It obtains its goods with 30 days trade credit from a wholesaler.
Explain **one** reason why the wholesaler would be interested in the balance sheet of QNB. [2]

The wholesaler would be interested in the balance sheet of QNB as it shows its ability to pay its debts through working capital[1] which will tell the wholesaler if the enterprise is likely to be able to pay them on time / helps the wholesaler to confidently agree trade credit and on what terms.[1]

SCENARIO

Helen owns and manages *Backstitch Ltd*, a women's tailor and alternations specialist. Helen has two employees and runs the enterprise from a rented shop space. The majority of sales in the first year of trading came via the enterprise's website. They also sell some new garments. However, Helen is now considering renting a larger warehouse as the shop space is becoming too small.

Figure 1 shows an extract from Helen's balance sheet.

(a) Using the data below, calculate *Backstitch's* working capital (net current assets). [1]

Extract from balance sheet (Statement of financial position)	£
Fixed assets	12 200
Current assets	7 500
Current liabilities	4 000

(b) Helen shows current assets and current liabilities on the balance sheet.
   (i)   Give **one** example of a current asset Helen might have. [1]
   (ii) Give **one** example of a current liability Helen might have. [1]
   (iii) Give **one** reason an enterprise may have problems with its net current assets. [1]

(c) Helen's retained profits from the year-end balance sheets for 2021 and 2022 are given below.

	2021	2022
Retained profit	£6 704	£8 633

Explain **one** reason why the retained profit figures may have increased. [2]

Example answers

(a) Working capital = Current assets – Current liabilities. 7 500 – 4 000 = £3 500.[1]

(b) (i)   Cash in bank, stock.[1] (ii) Overdraft, creditor.[1]

(iii) One from: Poor cash flow forecasting,[1] poor stock control,[1] unexpected costs/events,[1] ineffective use of trade credit,[1] poor chasing/control of debtors/monies owed.[1]

(c) 2022 may have been a more profitable year for Helen[1] so more profit was brought across from the P&L account.[1] Fewer dividends may have been paid out to shareholders in 2022[1] meaning that more profit was retained in the enterprise as these figures are calculated after dividends have been paid.[1] 2021 may have been a profitable year[1] which meant that more profits were retained and rolled over into 2022 so the enterprise started at a higher point.[1]

EXAMINATION PRACTICE

Scenario: *D-Books*

Devon runs a second-hand bookstore *D-Books* as a sole-trader. Devon specialises in first edition books and limited-edition publishers. *D-Books* has customers throughout the world, many of whom buy online without visiting the store. Devon currently rents premises; however, the landlord is increasing the rent and Devon is worried about their profitability.

1. Devon has the following costs:
    - Book stock
    - Company logo design
    - Heat, light and power
    - Phone bills
    - Wages

    Give **two** examples of running costs from the list above. [2]

2. Devon wants to know how *D-Books* is performing.

    Complete the profit and loss account (statement of comprehensive income) for *D-Books*. [4]

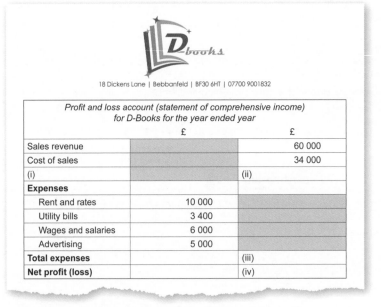

18 Dickens Lane | Bebbanfeld | BF30 6HT | 07700 9001832

Profit and loss account (statement of comprehensive income) for D-Books for the year ended year		
	£	£
Sales revenue		60 000
Cost of sales		34 000
(i)		(ii)
Expenses		
Rent and rates	10 000	
Utility bills	3 400	
Wages and salaries	6 000	
Advertising	5 000	
Total expenses		(iii)
Net profit (loss)		(iv)

3. Devon wants to increase sales revenue and decrease costs.
    (a) Explain **one** way Devon could increase *D-Books'* sales revenue. [2]
    (b) Explain **one** way Devon could decrease *D-Books'* costs. [2]

4. Accurate financial documents are required for stakeholders.
   Give **one** stakeholder of *D-Books*. [1]

5. Devon has provided a list of the current and long-term liabilities.

	£
Creditors	4 000
Mortgage	120 000
Overdraft	1 300
Tax payable	3 200

(a) Calculate the value of the **current liabilities** for *D-Books*. [2]

The top of *D-Books'* balance sheet is given below.

18 Dickens Lane | Bebbanfeld | BF30 6HT | 07700 9001832

Balance Sheet for D-Books as of 31st March 20XX	£	£
Fixed (non-current) assets		
Vehicle	4 000	
Equipment	1 200	
		5 200
Current assets		
Stock	14 000	
Cash	2 600	
Debtors	4 800	
		21 400
Total assets		26 600
Liabilities		
Current liabilities		

(b) Calculate the working capital for *D-Books*. [2]
   Use the following information to help you calculate your answer:
   - the values of the enterprise's liabilities in part (a)
   - the values of the enterprise's assets in the balance sheet.

PROFITABILITY AND LIQUIDITY

Cash and profit

Cash

Cash is defined as the **liquid assets** of an enterprise, including the bank balance. It appears as a current asset on an enterprise's balance sheet.

Profit

Profit is the difference that is left when costs are taken away from revenue. This appears on an enterprise's profit and loss account. Profit only becomes cash once any payments have been paid and cleared.

The difference between liquidity and profitability

Liquidity

Liquidity refers to an enterprise's ability to pay its debts. If an enterprise can pay its debts, it is **solvent** and has good liquidity. If an enterprise struggles to pay its debts it has poor liquidity and may become **insolvent**.

Profitability

Profitability refers to an enterprise's ability to turn revenue into profit. How much profit an enterprise can make often depends on its **profit margin**. This is the money it makes per item sold after all costs are removed.

Profitability ratios

A **ratio** compares one thing to another. Profitability ratios can be calculated using an enterprise's profit and loss account. There are two useful ratios to measure the profitability of an enterprise. These are the **gross profit margin** (**GPM**) and **net profit margin** (**NPM**).

Gross profit margin

Gross profit margin measures gross profit as a percentage of sales revenue. This shows the revenue that an enterprise can keep after all direct costs involved in production are covered.

Gross profit margin is calculated using the following formula:

$$\text{GPM} = \frac{\text{Gross profit}}{\text{Revenue}} \times 100$$

Example

$$\frac{93\,000}{150\,000} \times 100 = 62\%$$

This shows the enterprise has 62% revenue left after paying the direct costs.

Net profit margin

Net profit margin measures net profit as a percentage of sales revenue. This shows what the net profit is per £1 of sales made by the enterprise.

Net profit margin is calculated using the following formula:

$$\text{NPM} = \frac{\text{Net profit}}{\text{Revenue}} \times 100$$

Example

$$\frac{67\,500}{150\,000} \times 100 = 45\%$$

This shows the enterprise makes 0.45 of net income per £1 of sales.

Liquidity ratios

There are two useful ratios to measure the liquidity of an enterprise. These are the **current ratio** and the **liquid capital ratio**. The information used to calculate liquidity can be found on the balance sheet.

Current ratio

Current ratio measures the ability of an enterprise to pay debt. Although a useful ratio, an enterprise must be careful if it holds a lot of inventory as this can make the ratio misleading.

Current ratio is calculated using the following formula:

$$\text{Current ratio} = \frac{\text{Current assets}}{\text{Current liabilities}}$$

A healthy range is 1.5–3:1

Example

$$\frac{10\,000}{5\,000} = 2{:}1$$

This shows that for every £1 of liabilities an enterprise has, it has £2 in assets.

Liquid capital ratio

Liquid capital ratio also measures an enterprise's ability to pay debts. It is more accurate than the current ratio as it removes any inventory from its calculation.

Liquid capital ratio is calculated using the following formula:

$$\text{Liquid capital ratio} = \frac{\text{Current assets} - \text{Inventory}}{\text{Current liabilities}}$$

>1:1 is healthy

Example

$$\frac{10\,000 - 8\,000}{5\,000} = 0.4{:}1$$

This shows that for every £1 of liabilities an enterprise has, it has 40p in assets.

If stock can be quickly converted into cash, the current ratio may be most helpful. If the stock is difficult to sell quickly or if it may expire before sale (e.g. food or some medicines), the liquid capital ratio may be best.

Stakeholders and ratios

Ratios can be useful to stakeholders as they provide them with an overview of the performance of an enterprise.

Owners use profitability and liquidity ratios to understand how much profit they are making and how many assets they have compared to their liabilities. Owners can then take steps to improve underperforming areas, for example they may try to decrease costs to improve profitability.

Any investors will want to know how liquid or profitable an enterprise is so they can decide if they want to invest in an enterprise. Ratios can provide them with important performance indicators.

Managers will be interested as they can take actions to improve the profitability and liquidity alongside the owner. They are interested to know if targets have been met.

If the liquidity of an enterprise is poor, debts may become difficult to pay and a creditor might choose to refuse them credit because they are too much of a financial risk.

SCENARIO

Beccie is an Internet entrepreneur who runs *Healthy Body* specialising in vitamins and supplements to improve physical health and wellbeing.

1. (a) Explain **one** advantage to *Healthy Body* of selling online. [2]

Beccie needs to calculate the liquidity for *Healthy Body* as they increase debts due to expansion of the enterprise. Beccie uses the liquid capital ratio.

$$\text{Liquid Capital ratio} = \frac{\text{Current assets} - \text{Inventory}}{\text{Current liabilities}}$$

Inventory	£2 000
Current assets	£4 000
Current liabilities	£1 800

(b) Using the figures provided above, calculate the liquid capital ratio for *Healthy Body*. [1]
Show your working.

Beccie has calculated the profits for the enterprise's last year of trading.

$$\text{NPM} = \frac{\text{Net profit}}{\text{Revenue}} \times 100$$

Revenue	150 000
Net Profit	60 000

(c) Using the figures above, calculate the net profit margin for *Healthy Body*. [1]
Show your working.

2. Beccie is looking to increase *Healthy Body's* credit limit with their local supplier.

Explain **one** reason why their supplier might be interested in the liquidity ratios. [2]

Example answers

1. (a) *Operating online means Beccie increases her customer base[1] as she can reach a worldwide audience.[1] Beccie's enterprise can compete better[1] as online customers can order 24/7.[1] Costs can also be lowered / profits increased,[1] without the costs associated with a bricks and mortar shop.[1]*

   (b) *4 000 – 2 000 = 2 000. 2 000 ÷ 1 800 = 1.1:1[1]*   (c) *60 000 ÷ 150 000 = 0.4 . 0.4 × 100 = 40%[1]*

2. *Beccie's supplier might be interested in the liquidity ratios as they will want to check Healthy Body has enough assets to cover its liabilities [1] as they don't want run the risk of the enterprise not being able to pay them.[1]*

EXAMINATION PRACTICE

Daisy and Dorothy have run a flower shop called *Daisy Dot Flower Shop* for three years. Dorothy has recently received the profit and loss account. Daisy is interested to find out what their gross profit and net profit margins are.

1. (a) Using the accounts below, calculate the gross profit margin for *Daisy Dot Flower Shop*. [2]
    (b) Using the accounts below, calculate the net profit margin for *Daisy Dot Flower Shop*. [2]

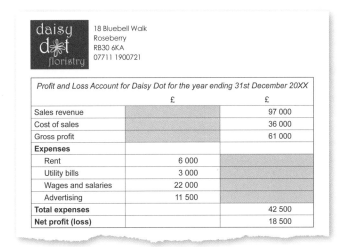

daisy
dot
floristry

18 Bluebell Walk
Roseberry
RB30 6KA
07711 1900721

Profit and Loss Account for Daisy Dot for the year ending 31st December 20XX

	£	£
Sales revenue		97 000
Cost of sales		36 000
Gross profit		61 000
Expenses		
Rent	6 000	
Utility bills	3 000	
Wages and salaries	22 000	
Advertising	11 500	
Total expenses		42 500
Net profit (loss)		18 500

(c) In year 1, the net profit margin was 14%. In year 2 the net profit margin was 17%.

Using your answer for part (b), explain how the enterprise has been doing over the three-year period. [2]

(d) Explain **two** actions *Daisy Dot* could take to improve the enterprise's net profit margin. [2]

2. Dorothy calculates the enterprise's liquidity before considering any additional spend on marketing.

(a) Explain why Dorothy might do this. [2]

(b) Explain why *Daisy Dot* may prefer to use the liquid capital ratio rather than the current ratio to calculate its liquidity.

(c) Explain **one** action *Daisy Dot* could take to improve its liquidity. [2]

BUDGETING

The purpose of a **budget** is to help an enterprise plan future expenditure and revenues with the main aim of ensuring that the enterprise is able to make a profit. Budgets can be based on the money an enterprise spends or the number of sales, or revenue, it seeks to make.

Budgets should be set carefully using any financial information that is available so that they are as accurate as possible.

Expenditure and revenue budgets

Capital expenditure

A **capital expenditure** budget is usually reserved for fixed assets such as large machinery or premises. As these purchases are usually expensive, they have a separate budget.

Cash

A **cash** budget monitors the inflow and outflows of cash over time. Its purpose is to show all the planned monthly cash incomings and cash outgoings. It helps an enterprise to manage its cash flow.

Labour

A **labour** budget is set to pay for the employees in an enterprise. It takes into account how much it costs to achieve production or service aims and objectives, and how much labour is needed.

Marketing and promotion

A **marketing** or **promotional** budget is used to promote the enterprise and its goods or services. The marketing budget is an estimate of the costs required to market the enterprise successfully.

Revenue and sales

A **revenue** or **sales** budget estimates how much revenue an enterprise might generate over a period of time.

To do this, an enterprise should focus on the number of products they might sell and how much they might sell them for. This allows an enterprise to predict how they might perform.

Production

Production budgets are based on the amount of product that needs to be provided or manufactured. In order for an enterprise to estimate this accurately, they need to consider a projection of how many units the enterprise might sell over a certain period and work out how much this will cost to produce.

Overheads

An **overheads** budget calculates what it costs to run an enterprise. This includes rent, insurance and utility bills. Operating expenses are required to run an enterprise and cannot be avoided.

Purchases and materials

Purchase and **materials** budgets are set and used to purchase any raw materials or other resources an enterprise might need in order to produce goods or services.

Difference between budgeting and budgetary control

Once a **budget** has been set, there must be a way to monitor the targets. This is known as **budgetary control**. Budgetary control is a process which involves regularly checking an enterprise's performance and spending against the budgetary plan. Control procedures bring things back in line if expected budgets are being exceeded or if things are not going as planned.

Impact of favourable or adverse variances

Budgets can be subjected to either favourable or adverse variances. A variance is a difference between actual and budgeted figures. A **favourable variance** shows when the actual budget result is better than expected. For example, costs might be lower than expected in the overhead budget or revenue was higher than expected in the sales budget. An **adverse variance** indicates where the actual budget result is worse than expected. This might mean that costs were higher than expected, for example labour costs might have increased or revenue was lower than expected.

Alexandros owns a Greek restaurant with 10 employees. There are often too many employees on shift when the restaurant is quiet. The enterprise has not set a labour budget.

(a) Give **one** reason why an enterprise would want to set a labour budget. [1]

(b) Alexandros has calculated that he requires each employee to work an average of 24 hours per week on an average wage of £14 per hour.
Calculate Alexandros' labour budget for the next 26 weeks. [2]

(c) Discuss the impacts on Alexandros of a limited marketing budget. [6]

(a) To make sure the enterprise is not overspending on staff.[1]
To make sure that the enterprise manages its staffing within its needs.[1]

(b) 24 × 14 = 336.[1] 336 × 26 × 10 employees = £87 360.[1] Allow one mark for correct workings.

(c) A limited promotional budget will help limit the spending on promotion which could reduce costs and increase overall profits. A budget provides a scope for employees responsible for promotion to work within, so this helps Alexandros to manage spending and control output.

Alexandros will need to consider the choice of promotional methods, but the budget may limit those choices. A limited budget may mean that less expensive promotional methods are required, which may be less effective. Reduced budgets may mean that the right promotional methods for the enterprise's brand image become unaffordable, which may put people off using the restaurant if less expensive marketing 'cheapens' the brand. Market research methods may be included in this budget, but may be limited according to cost which may limit the suitability or reach.
This question should be marked in accordance with the levels of response guidance on page 75.

Alexandros

CASH FLOW

A cash flow forecast is a prediction of the inflows and outflows of money into an enterprise over a period of time

Cash flow forecast

An enterprise's inflows and outflows of money indicate whether they have positive or negative liquidity. In other words, will there be sufficient cash coming in to cover the running costs?

The purpose of cash flow forecasts is as follows:

- To identify what monies the enterprise has coming in and going out over time. This usually includes the value and the various sources or beneficiaries.

- To examine the impact that the timings of the inflows and outflows might have on an enterprise.

- To determine periods of potential positive and negative liquidity, to help the enterprise to make business decisions. For example, if an enterprise forecasts negative liquidity they may be able to address the issue before it happens in real time by, for example, cutting back on spending, postponing a payment or calling in debtors earlier. Similarly, if an enterprise identifies that it might have strong positive liquidity, it can decide if it wants to spend a little more money, for example, on stock or promotion, for that period if the forecast is accurate.

Cash flow statement

A **cash flow statement** shows the **actual** inflows and outflows of money into an enterprise rather than a prediction. It provides a detailed picture of what has happened to an enterprise's cash inflows and outflows over a given period – usually 1 year. This can help make cash flow forecasts in the future more accurate as the enterprise has something to base forecasts on.

Elements of a cash flow forecast/statement

Predicted and actual cash inflows or receipts

Predicted cash inflows or receipts are the monies that an enterprise expects to come into its bank account each month. They are likely to be predicted based on previous sales history or pre-orders. Inflows can come from revenue, share capital, bank loans or rent. **Actual inflows** are the monies into the enterprise the company actually receives. These appear on a cash flow statement.

Predicted and actual outflows or payments

Predicted cash outflows or payments are the monies that an enterprise forecasts it is likely to have to pay out each month. These may be predicted based on previous expenditure, for example, bills and salaries, or on other factors, for example, a plan to buy new machinery. Outflows can include wages, utility bills, purchases of materials, loan repayments, marketing, rent, insurance and many other things. **Actual outflows** are what the enterprise has actually paid out. These appear on a cash flow statement.

Net inflows and outflows

Net Inflows and outflows are the total inflows and outflows an enterprise has. It is calculated as total inflows less total outflows. This indicates if an enterprise has more money coming in than is going out or vice versa. It helps the enterprise to identify if there is a cash flow problem. An enterprise needs to know how much cash is flowing in and out so it can make sure it can afford any purchases it needs to make and can also cover its bills.

Opening and closing balances

Opening and closing balances show what an enterprise started with in terms of cash at the beginning of a month and what cash they had at the end of the month. The closing balance on the last day of every month is always carried forward to the next monthly period.

Surpluses and deficits

An enterprise will want to know at the end of the month that it has received enough inflows to balance its outflow cash spending. If an enterprise has more cash coming in than going out they will have a cash **surplus**. This is referred to as **positive cash flow**. If an enterprise has more cash going out than coming in this is called a **deficit**. This is referred to as **negative cash flow**.

Example

This is an example of a cash flow forecast for *Carpet Care*, a carpet cleaning and repair enterprise, covering the first quarter of the year. All cash inflows and outflows are predictions.

Money flowing **into** the enterprise

Money flowing **out** of the enterprise

Closing balance of the month is always the opening balance of the next month.

Cash Flow Forecast for Carpet Care for the first quarter in 20XX			
	January (£)	February (£)	March (£)
CASH INFLOWS			
Contract sales	300.00	500.00	450.00
One-off services	130.00	200.00	300.00
Business loan	5 000.00	-	-
Total inflows	5 430.00	700.00	750.00
CASH OUTFLOWS			
Cleaning equipment	3 000.00	-	-
Detergents and consumables	50.00	80.00	100.00
Fuel and van maintenance	200.00	400.00	350.00
Loan repayment	-	400.00	400.00
Total outflows	3 250.00	880.00	850.00
NET INFLOWS / OUTFLOWS	2 180.00	(180.00)	(100.00)
Opening balance	100.00	2 280.00	2 100.00
Closing balance	2 280.00	2 100.00	2 000.00

Explain the impact of the loan on *Carpet Care* over the three month period. [2]

The loan in January will give Carpet Care surplus cash flow[1] which can compensate for a cash flow deficit in February and March.[1]
Carpet will should have negative net cash flow in February and March owing to the addition of the loan repayments[1] with £2000 closing balance carried over into April.[1]

SUGGESTING IMPROVEMENTS TO CASH FLOW PROBLEMS

An enterprise should undertake a cash flow forecast to help avoid cash flow problems. Both **positive** and **negative cash flow** will impact an enterprise.

Impacts of positive and negative cash flow

Positive cash flow

Positive cash flow is good for an enterprise as this means it is able to pay for all its outflows without having liquidity problems. Having positive cash flow, however, may mean the enterprise is not spending enough on stock or promotion, and may find this increases its spending later.

Negative cash flow

Negative cash flow indicates a financial health problem for the enterprise as it is paying more money out per month than it has coming in. An enterprise will need to identify each inflow and outflow on a cash flow forecast, and then take measures to stop this happening.

Cash flow problems

Cash surpluses

A **cash surplus** means an enterprise has more cash coming in than going out at the end of the month. This shows good financial health. However, if this happens continually and the surplus grows, any investors might question why this cash is not being put to good use.

Having a cash surplus means the enterprise has spare cash to spend in the event of an emergency or, if, for example it needs to employ more staff.

1. Give **two** benefits to an enterprise of having a cash surplus. [2]

   It helps them to grow the enterprise using this surplus if they want to.[1] They can pay their bills comfortably/on time.[1] They can order stock or invest money in trying different products.[1]

Cash deficits

A **cash deficit** means that an enterprise has more cash leaving the enterprise than it has coming in over a period. This shows a problem for the enterprise.

When cash outflows exceed cash inflows, enterprises may struggle to pay debts and other expenses. This would be concerning to an investor as they may think the enterprise is not making enough money to cover debts. Owners would be worried about how to maintain the enterprise's future and seek alternative funding or cash flow solutions. Managers would also be concerned about their job security and finding solutions.

Deficits can come from poor record keeping, having too many bills over a set period, unexpected costs or debtors not paying on time.

Many enterprises fail owing to cash flow issues — often they try to grow too quickly which may cause costs to exceed revenues.

Solutions to cash flow problems

Selling off unused assets / inventory

If an enterprise has fixed assets or old stock which are underused or not used at all, it might consider selling these in order to generate cash.

Reducing the credit period offered to customers

Credit terms for customers could be reduced, for example, from 60 days to 30 days to ensure an enterprise receives payment more quickly. This could, however, create a competitive disadvantage and lead to a loss of custom if a competitor is able to offer better terms elsewhere.

Chasing debtors for monies owed

An enterprise should chase debtors to ensure timely payments and boost inflow. They may also restrict credit to late paying debtors, forcing them to pay at the time of purchase in future.

Delaying payment to suppliers

Some suppliers may agree to a delayed payment. However, this is a risky strategy as suppliers may stop supplying the enterprise or refuse to supply credit, leading to further cash flow problems.

Solutions to cash flow problems

Increasing revenue

An enterprise can improve revenue by raising prices or using a sales promotion to increase volume.

Cutting costs

Unnecessary expenditure can be reduced to improve cash flow.

Paying off debts

An enterprise might consider paying off any debts, for example by obtaining a bank loan or by selling any fixed or current assets. This may be a short-term solution, but the enterprise has either reduced its assets or increased its long-term liabilities, adding loan repayments to its future outflows.

Cutting back or delaying expansion plans

Any expansion plans could be delayed or reduced until cash flow improves. Doing this could free up cash which could be used to pay more immediate outgoings.

---

2. Give **two** ways in which a cash deficit may occur. [2]

Sales may be lower than expected.[1]
Expenses may be greater than expected.[1]
Suppliers may stop allowing credit.[1]
Customers may be slow to pay their invoices.[1] Owners may take too much money out of the enterprise.[1] Too much money is tied up in assets / stock.[1]

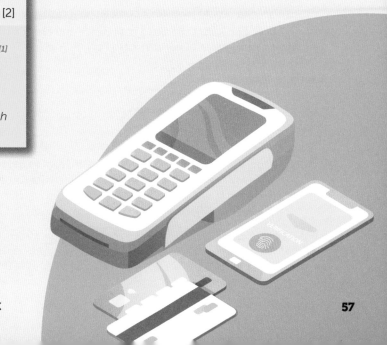

Anita owns a sole trader enterprise called *Makeup Surprises*, specialising in mystery gift boxes of makeup items. Customers purchase these from an online store and Anita ships them via Royal Mail. There are three box sizes each containing different valued items. These are priced at £20, £40 and £70. Promotion is done entirely through social media. Anita is considering expanding the mystery box lines and is interested in making a forecast of the enterprise's cash flow for the next few months.

1. Give **two** budgets that Anita might use for the enterprise.   [2]

2. Anita needs to create a cash flow forecast.

Cash flow forecast for Makeup Surprises for the final quarter in 20XX.			
	October (£)	November (£)	December (£)
CASH INFLOWS			
Total inflows	6 000	5 000	2 500
CASH OUTFLOWS			
Total outflows	4 000	2 000	7 000
NET INFLOWS / OUTFLOWS	(i)	3 000	(4 500)
Opening balance	5 000	(iii)	10 000
Closing balance	(ii)	10 000	(iv)

(a) Complete the cash flow forecast for October–December.   [4]
(b) Explain **one** benefit to Anita of completing a cash flow forecast.   [2]
(c) In December, Anita observed a cash deficit and predicts a negative closing balance in January. Explain **one** impact of negative cash flow on *Makeup Surprises*.   [2]

Example answers

1. *Two from: Cash budget,[1] marketing/promotion budget,[1] overheads budget,[1] purchases/materials budget,[1] sales budget.[1] Labour budget would not be valid as she works alone.*

2. (a) *(i) 2 000,[1] (ii) 7 000,[1] (iii) 7 000,[1] 5 500.[1]*

    (b) *It is beneficial for Anita to complete a cash flow forecast as Makeup Surprises needs to predict if it will have any cash shortfalls in the future[1] so Anita can put measures in place (e.g. reduce spending) to avoid cash flow problems in the future.[1] Cash flow forecasts help Makeup Surprises to manage its liquidity[1] so it can comfortably fund its expenses in future.[1]*

    (c) *Negative cash flow will make it difficult to pay suppliers[1] so Anita may need to look into short-term loans or investment to manage the shortfall.[1] There will be no cash available for expansion[1] so Anita may need to shelve plans, slowing the growth of the enterprise.[1]*

EXAMINATION PRACTICE

Scenario: *MJK Builders*

Marvin is a local builder running an enterprise called *MJK Builders*. Marvin currently has four employees and owns two vehicles as well as a small warehouse. Marvin have already produced a capital expenditure and a labour budget and a sales budget for *MJK Builders'* estimated revenues.

1. (a) Give **two** other budgets that would be useful for *MJK Builders* to produce.   [2]
    (b) Explain **one** benefit to Marvin of producing a sales budget.   [2]

2. To help Marvin manage the enterprise, he uses budgetary control. This helps Marvin to compare planned budgets with actual budgets to identify any differences.
    Marvin identifies an adverse labour variance.
    (a) Give the meaning of an adverse labour variance.   [1]
    (b) Explain **one** way in which identifying this variance will help Marvin to manage the enterprise.   [2]

3. Marvin applies for a loan as he wants to expand the enterprise. The bank has asked Marvin to provide overhead, labour and sales budgets.
    For each budget explain **one** reason why the bank may have asked Marvin to provide these figures.   [6]

    Overhead budget   Labour budget   Sales budget

4. Marvin has developed a cash flow forecast for the next quarter.

	April (£)	May (£)	June (£)
Total inflows	23 150	18 200	27 200
Total outflows	16 210	26 100	29 900
Net cash flow	6 940	(ii)	(2 700)
Opening balance	3 000	9 940	(iii)
Closing balance	(i)	2 040	(iv)

    (a) Complete the cash flow forecast for *MJK Builders*.   [4]
    (b) Explain **one** way that *MJK Builders* can improve their cash flow.   [2]

BREAK-EVEN

Break-even analysis

Break-even analysis is a planning tool that indicates how many products an enterprise needs to sell and at what cost in order to break even.

Break-even point

The break-even point is where the revenue an enterprise receives is equal to its costs. It is the point at which an enterprise neither makes a profit or a loss.

> The break-even point is always measured in units, and never in pounds and pence.

The **break-even point** can be calculated using the following formula:

Break-even point: Fixed costs ÷ (selling price − variable costs)

The break-even point demonstrates the number of units an enterprise must sell in order to cover costs. If an enterprise sells fewer than this number, it will make a loss. If it sells more than this number, it will make a profit.

An enterprise must break even in order to cover its costs and continue to trade.

1. Simon Head runs *Head Cases Ltd*, selling mobile phone cases online. Calculate the break-even point based on the following figures. Selling price £10, variable cost £6, fixed costs £16 000. [2]

   10 − 6 = 4, £16 000 ÷ 4 = 4 000 units.[2] *One mark for correct workings only.*

Margin of safety

The **margin of safety** (**MOS**) is the difference between the break-even point and the actual sales of an enterprise. Any revenue that takes an enterprise above the break-even point can be considered the margin of safety. It is essentially a cushion allowing an enterprise to see how many extra units above the break-even point it is selling and how safe it is from making a loss.

The margin of safety can be calculated using the following formula:

Margin of safety: Estimated sales − break-even point

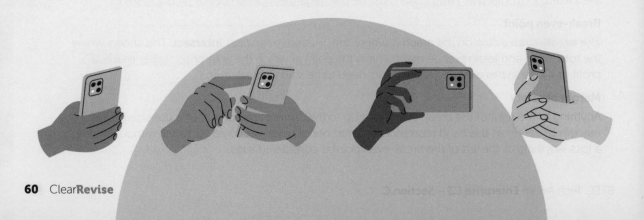

Constructing a break-even chart

Enterprises can draw a break-even chart to show visually how many products the enterprise needs to sell in order to break even. The fixed costs, variable costs and unit selling price are required to construct this chart.

Example

> Remember that the break-even point is where the upper two lines cross.
>
> Forgetting to label your lines could cost you the marks.

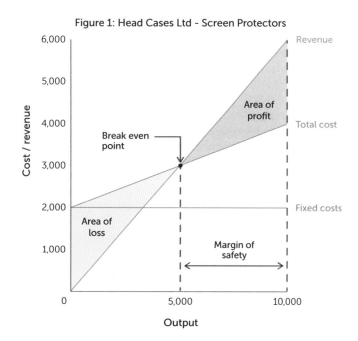

Figure 1: Head Cases Ltd - Screen Protectors

Revenue

Revenue is the **green** line. This shows how much income is coming into the enterprise. It starts at 0 as no sales means no income. To calculate revenue, the enterprise must multiply the number sold by the sales price.

Total costs

The **red** line shows the total costs of the enterprise. This is calculated by adding together the **fixed costs** and the **variable costs**. A variable cost is one that changes with output. The total costs line starts at the fixed cost line. This is because an enterprise must still pay fixed costs even if it only sells one unit.

Fixed costs

The **purple** line shows the **fixed costs** for the enterprise. As these do not change with output, they are a fixed horizontal line. Fixed costs must be paid regardless of number of products sold.

Break-even point

The **break-even point** on the graph is where the **red** and **green** lines **intersect**. This shows where the total costs and total revenue meet. This is the point at which the enterprise neither makes a profit or a loss. In this example, 5 000 units need to be sold to break even.

Margin of safety

Anything to the right of the break-even point up to the current level of output is considered the **margin of safety** as this band represents the number of units that could fail to sell without incurring a loss. Anything to the left of the break-even point is considered a loss.

2. Study the break-even chart for a range of new screen protectors for *Head Cases Ltd* in Figure 1. Explain how an increase in rent costs would impact the break-even point. [2]

3. (a) Calculate the margin of safety if Simon sells 6 500 screen protectors. [1]

   (b) Give **one** reason why knowing the margin of safety is important to Simon. [1]

   (c) Explain why it is important for an enterprise to break even. [2]

2. *The break-even point would be higher / more sales would be required to break even[1] because the fixed costs would increase causing the total costs line to move upwards.[1]*

3. *(a) 6 500 – 5 000 = 1 500.[1]*

   (b) It will indicate how many sales can be lost before making a loss / reduce the risk of making a loss.[1]

   (c) An enterprise must break even to continue trading[1] unless they have additional funding to cover the deficit.[1]
   Below this point, they will have negative liquidity[1] which could eventually result in closure.[1]

Strengths and limitations of a break-even analysis

Break even analysis can be very useful for the following reasons:

- An enterprise can calculate its potential sales revenue at each level of output.
- It can show if a product is worth selling or if it is too risky.
- An enterprise knows its fixed and variable costs, so the number of items needing to be sold to break even and make a profit becomes known.
- The margin of safety can be calculated.
- An enterprise can experiment with pricing to find the best price for its product with the lowest break-even point.
- An enterprise can act to reduce the break-even point e.g. by cutting costs or raising prices.
- An enterprise can experiment with 'what if' scenarios to see what happens to the break-even point if prices or costs change.
- It is quick and easy to analyse.

Despite these benefits, the tool is not without limitations:

- Break even analysis assumes all things stay the same. For example, all stock is sold at a set price or costs remain the same.
- It presumes only one product is sold. If an enterprise produces several products, it is very difficult for it to calculate the break-even point.
- The enterprise may buy in bulk and receive a discount. Costs will decrease or vary, however this cannot be shown on the break-even chart as costs and revenues are shown as a line.
- Enterprises can be unrealistic in their calculations, meaning any break-even analysis is less useful.
- Charts can be time consuming to create, particularly if the enterprise is using it to identify 'what-if' scenarios.

SCENARIO

Peter and Jack are fishermen on the Cornish coast. They run an enterprise called *Cold Sea Supplies*. They specialise in catching lobsters using pots but are interested in growing the enterprise to catch crabs as well.

They would like to know how many crabs they would need to catch each week to break even.

Figure 1 shows some estimated costs and revenues for this venture:

1. Using the data in the table below, draw and label the break-even chart. You must draw and label:

   • the fixed costs line, the total costs line, and the total revenue line.

   You must also label:
   • the break-even point. [4]

Costs and revenues for *Cold Sea Supplies* each week				
Number of units	0	1 000	2 000	3 000
Sales revenue	£0	£4 000	£8 000	£12 000
Fixed costs	£2 000	£2 000	£2 000	£2 000
Total costs	£2 000	£4 000	£6 000	£8 000

2. Calculate *Cold Sea Supplies'* margin of safety if they sell 3 000 crabs. [2]

Example answers

1.

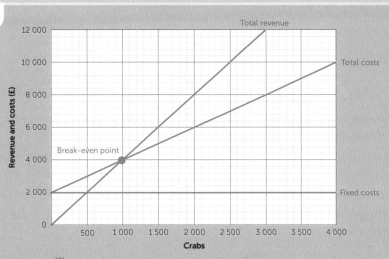

2. 3000 – 1 000 = 2 000 crabs[2]

SOURCES OF BUSINESS FINANCE

All enterprises need sources of finance to set up the enterprise and to continue to run it as a going concern.

Key considerations for finance

Different sources of finance will be used depending on the purpose and needs of the enterprise. For example, a mortgage may be taken if an enterprise wishes to own premises rather than lease them. Similarly, if an enterprise is just starting out, it may need a loan or it could use personal funds depending on amount of money needed and for what purpose.

When deciding which kind of finance to use, an enterprise should consider the following factors:
- What amount of finance is needed?
- What the finance will be used for and how long?
- How much the finance will cost the enterprise?
- What benefit will it receive from obtaining the finance?
- What is the borrowing term (duration) and the interest rate?
- Will the enterprise operations need to change in order to pay back the funds? For instance, price rises or reduced costs.

Internal sources of finance

Internal sources of finance come from sources close to the enterprise. These are usually preferred as there is less cost to the enterprise compared to external methods.

Personal sources

For example: (savings, credit cards, borrowing from friends and family).

Advantages
- Savings – No interest to pay.
- Credit card – Can take advantage of 0% interest rates for new card holders.
- Borrowing from family – Usually no or low interest payable.

Disadvantages
- Savings – If the enterprise fails, the owner loses the money.
- Credit card – If the finance cannot be paid back in time, then a higher interest rate will apply.
- Can only borrow to the 'limit' of the card.
- Borrowing from family – May insist the money is paid back at any point which could harm the enterprise.

Retained profits (Profits from the enterprise)

Advantages
- Money does not have to be repaid so no interest is applied.

Disadvantages
- Many enterprises have insufficient retained profits to reinvest back into the enterprise.

Sale of assets (Things the enterprise owns)

Advantages
- A good way to raise money from selling older assets no longer needed.
- Can avoid a loan and the associated interest payments.

Disadvantages
- Some enterprises may not have assets to sell especially if they are a start up enterprise.
- Assets can take a long time to sell.

EXTERNAL SOURCES OF FINANCE

External sources of finance include banks, institutions, individuals and companies outside of the enterprise.

Long-term

	Advantages	Disadvantages
Mortgage	• Cost effective way of borrowing. • No empty money towards rent.	• Will pay a lot more back than you originally borrowed. • Difficult for some enterprises to raise a deposit to access a mortgage.
Share capital	• Any money raised through shares can be used by the enterprise however it wants. • No repayment requirements.	• Selling shares reduces the control and ownership of an enterprise. • Shareholders expect a return on their investment (dividend).
Taking on new partners	• Can gain new ideas and skill sets. • Shared risks.	• May have disagreements. • Less profit as it will need to be split more ways.

Medium-term

	Advantages	Disadvantages
Hire Purchase (HP)	• Can pay in instalments so it is more affordable. • Will own the asset at the end of the payment term.	• It is more expensive to buy an asset this way compared to buying outright. • Defaulting on payment may mean the asset can be repossessed.
Leasing	• Enterprise can loan expensive equipment without having to buy it. • Can schedule how long the lease is for, so it doesn't waste money.	• The enterprise will not own the asset. • Leasing can be more expensive over the longer term than buying an asset or using HP.
Loans (usually from the bank or building society)	• The interest rate is usually fixed for the entire loan period. • Easy to budget as it is a fixed cost every month.	• Interest rates may be high. • Failure to repay the loan may lead to bankruptcy and repossession of assets. • Bank may want security (e.g. a fixed asset) to loan against.
Peer to Peer lending (P2P)	• It can be useful for some enterprises that do not have good credit ratings or struggle to get loans. • Quick to get money as most lenders have a waiting list of investors. • Convenient online applications.	• Interest repayments need to be paid. • Commonly involve an arrangement fee. • Enterprise needs to pass a credit check and other internal checks. • Initial amount borrowed needs to be paid at the end of the loan period.
Business angel investment	• Can also provide a source of advice and support. • Do not have to pay interest or repayments.	• May involve allowing them to make management decisions and/or giving them a share of the enterprise.

	Advantages	Disadvantages
Bank overdraft (a type of short term loan from the bank)	• Quick access to finance. • Flexible method of getting finance as and when required.	• Has a high rate of interest if it is not agreed in advance. • Has to be repaid quickly.
Crowdfunding	• Quick way to raise finance with no fees. • Alternative source if enterprises struggle to get bank loans. • Investors can help make suggestions to make the enterprise stronger.	• If you don't reach the funding target, money is returned to the investors. • If you don't own copyright or a patent someone can steal your idea. • Need to invest time and money to launch the project.
Trade credit	• Helps with cash flow as you can 'buy now and pay later', helping to generate the cash to pay for the finance. • No interest is payable.	• Credit has to be agreed with the supplier and they can withdraw this at any time. • Can only be used with certain suppliers.

Other

	Advantages	Disadvantages
Government and charitable grants	• Grants do not need paying back.	• Only certain types of enterprises are eligible for these. • May be conditions attached to them which have to be fulfilled.

Briston Riding School purchases animal feed from its supplier who allows them to make payment at anytime within 30 days.

Give the name of this source of finance. [1]

Trade credit. [1]

SCENARIO

Jan and Eric run a garden centre called *Handy Plants*. They have decided they would like to purchase a van to offer a delivery service to the local community. Jan and Eric only bought the garden centre last year so purchasing a van is going to be a large, medium-term expense for them.

Discuss the factors *Handy Plants* might need to consider when deciding which source of finance to use.　　　　　　　　　　　　　　　　　　　　　　　　　　　　　　　[6]

Example answers

Responses will be credited according to the learner's demonstration of knowledge and understanding of the material, using the indicative content and level descriptors below.

The indicative content that follows is not prescriptive. Responses may cover some or all indicative content, but learners should be rewarded for other relevant responses.

Indicative content:

- *How much savings do they have? Can they afford to buy the van outright? This would be the best option for them as they will be able to buy it without any interest repayments.*
- *Can they use retained profit? Unlikely as they have only owned the garden centre since last year. However similarly to buying outright, this will not cost them in terms of interest repayments, however it might take vital cash out of the young enterprise that they need to use elsewhere, for example, for stock or expansion.*
- *Consider leasing. Handy Plants can use the van for the time they want and return it afterwards. Jan and Eric may not want to do this as they are offering a delivery service and are likely to need the van long term. With leasing they will never physically own the asset.*
- *HP may be an option. This allows them to pay for the van in instalments, meaning the total cost can be spread out for them. However, this is more costly than the original van price due to the interest charge, and if they miss payments, the van can be repossessed.*
- *If they have good credit scores, a bank loan may work out cheaper than HP so they could obtain a bank loan, pay outright for the van, then pay the bank back in instalments. They will, however, still need to pay interest on these repayments and failure to pay will result in secured assets being repossessed.*

A conclusion is not required for a 'discuss' question.
Long answers must be written in paragraphs. We have used bullet points here to make the answers easier to understand.
This type of question will be marked using a Levels Based Marks Scheme. See page 75 for details.

EXAMINATION PRACTICE

Scenario: *Intruder Scan Ltd*

Rosie owns a local home security enterprise with partner Jack called *Intruder Scan Ltd*.

Intruder Scan Ltd charges £850 per basic alarm system install. Rosie would like to improve the break-even point by increasing the price of their service to £990.

1. Figure 1 shows some estimated costs and revenues if they increase their price to £990.

Costs and revenues for *Intruder Scan Ltd* each month				
Number of installations	0	10	20	30
Sales revenue	£0	£9 900	£19 800	£29 700
Fixed costs	£5 600	£5 600	£5 600	£5 600
Total costs	£5 600	£8 390	£11 450	£14 510

(a) Using the data in Figure 1, draw and label the break-even chart. You must draw and label:
• the fixed costs line • the total costs line • the total revenue line.
You must also label the break-even point [4]

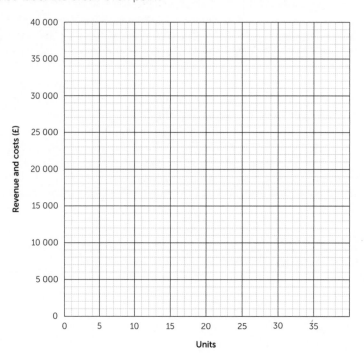

(b) Jack is interested in finding out about margin of safety.

    (i)   Calculate the margin of safety if Jack installs 20 alarm systems in one month.   [2]

    (ii) Give **one** reason why knowing the margin of safety would be important for *Intruder Scan Ltd*.   [1]

(c) Jack has left out the costs of travel to an installation so needs to allow more money to cover this additional cost.
Explain **one** way this increase in variable costs of travel would affect the break-even point.   [2]

(d) Explain **one** reason why it is important for *Intruder Scan Ltd* to use break even analysis.   [1]

Rosie would like to calculate the break-even point if the enterprise was to hire an additional employee so they could cut double the number of installations each month.

The enterprise has given you the new estimated figures for a month of trading.
- Fixed costs £7 800
- Variable costs for each job £279
- Selling price for each job £990

The formula used to calculate the break-even point for each job is:

Break-even point = Fixed costs / (selling price − variable cost)

(e) Using the figures given above, calculate the break-even point for the addition of the employee.   [1]

(f) Based on these figures, explain if Rosie should hire the additional employee.   [2]

2. *Intruder Scan Ltd* purchase alarm components from a local manufacturer which allows them to purchase the goods and pay 30 days later.

(a) Give the name of this type of finance.   [1]

(b) Explain why this type of finance is beneficial to a small enterprise.   [2]

Rosie has recently been contacted by the landlord who intends to increase the rent of their warehouse premises by 25%, starting next month. Rosie is concerned about how this will affect their profitability and cash flow. After speaking with Jack, they have decided to consider if it would be more beneficial for them to purchase premises or continue to rent the existing premises.

After speaking with the bank regarding purchasing the premises the costs per month of each option are as follows:
- Rent £590 per month
- Mortgage on new premises £610 per month

(c) Evaluate whether Rosie and Jack should continue to rent or purchase a new premises for their enterprise.   [6]

EXAMINATION PRACTICE ANSWERS

(a)   The enterprise is offering a specialised service. [1] Sky diving is usually a hobby /not everyone wants to sky dive. [1]   [1]

(b)   Two from: psychographically by attitudes and lifestyles. [1] Demographic segmentation by age, [1] socio-economic group, [1] or income. [1] Behavioural segmentation. [1]   [2]

(c)   Segmenting the market identifies which groups may buy an enterprise's products (1) which means that it can create the right advertisements / offer services more relevant to customers / develop its brand to appeal to customers. [1]
Market segmentation divides the market into specific groups to be targeted (1) so this may help the enterprise to gain a competitive advantage [1] by targeting advertising more effectively.   [2]

(d)   Geographical segmentation would allow *Pineham Indoor Sky Diving* to identify the number of likely customers / needs and wants of people in the area they are looking to expand into [1] so that they can create demand in these areas. [1]   [2]

(e)   The enterprise could record the details of each customer and each visit. [1] Then use this data to calculate an average usage / number of visits per customer over time. [1]
The enterprise could offer a loyalty scheme [1] which would allow it to see how often people visited the business. [1]   [2]

(f)   Indicative content may include:
Advantages of B2B trading:
*   The B2B market would open up a large and potentially profitable new segment.
*   Workplace outings / teambuilding events could be popular / could get interest from regular / large profitable group bookings.
*   May increase trading during the days when most B2C customers will be at work.

Disadvantages of B2B trading:
*   The B2B market has different requirements such as the approaches to marketing which would need more time to research and implement.
*   May increase the costs of marketing and hospitality.
*   May need to develop their website to accommodate enterprise group bookings and information.   [6]

(g)   Indicative content may include:
Advantages of offering premium packages to people in higher socio-economic groups:
*   May be able to increase revenue as people have more disposable income.
*   Premium packages and services may have a greater profit margin, or could attract more add-on sales.
*   Teenagers living in more affluent families may be attracted and spread the word at schools / colleges.

Disadvantages of offering premium packages to people in higher socio-economic groups:
*   As it is a niche product, it might be a waste of money trying to attract people if they are not interested.
*   Those in higher socio-economic groups or those with more disposable income could include those later in their lives who have had successful working lives, and these people may not fit the demographic profile of a typical customer.
*   Premium packages may create demand for services that *Pineham Indoor Sky Diving* can't offer for example, closing the centre for exclusive access, which may be difficult to arrange.

Advantages of targeting the nearby university to attract students:
*   Students may fit the demographic profile of the average customer well.
*   Groups of students may book in their accommodation groups / class or friendship groups / sports teams which may increase larger, more profitable bookings.
*   Students may be willing/able to attend at non-peak times which may help to increase business during those periods.

Disadvantages of targeting the nearby university to attract students in neighbouring towns:
*   May need to use offers and discounts to attract them which may mean it does not make as much money as it would from regular customers.
*   University students are usually only there during term time. Therefore, there may be little custom from this group of students during the holidays.
*   The students who use the enterprise may only use it for a short amount of time, and as they leave the university, they will relocate meaning *Pineham Indoor Sky Diving* has to continually work hard to attract the next cohort of students.   [6]

Answers to 'discuss' and 'evaluate' questions must be written in paragraphs. We have used bullet points here to make the answers easier to understand. This type of question will be marked using a Levels Based Marks Scheme as provided on page 75.

(a) Zara has used multi-channel marketing. [1]

(b) Two from: Sponsorship, public relations, personal selling, trade shows, social media marketing. [2]

(c) Below the line promotion is usually less costly [1] which means they can direct more funds to be used elsewhere in the enterprise. [1]

An enterprise can narrow the focus for its promotion [1] which can help to reach the target market more effectively [1] leading to potential increase in sales. [4]

(d) (i) The new target market will have particular demographic and psychographic profiles which will need to be carefully matched to the right promotion method [1] so that the advertising appeals and is effective in order to increase the sales of the enterprise. [1] [2]

(ii) A budget of £500 will affect Zara as this is a relatively small amount of money [1] and will limit the methods the enterprise can choose / effectiveness. [1] This may limit things to only one method of promotion [1] which will restrict Zara's ability to capture the target audience's attention. [1] Cheaper promotion methods may be required [1] which may negatively affect the brand image / not fit with the brand image. [1] [2]

(e) Increasing a product range helps to spread risk because if the bakery sales start to decline, they may fall back on the new lunchtime sandwich line [1] to maintain or increase sales levels. [1]

An increase in products will increase choice [1] which can be a benefit to the consumer and increase sales / basket value. [1]

Existing customers may pick up additional sandwich items for their family or tell their family about the new products through word-of-mouth promotion [1] which would increase overall sales / profit. [1] [2]

(f) Potential customers will see the enterprise has sponsored the event, providing a positive public image [1] and increase brand awareness / sales. [1] Customer retention may increase [1] as they can see they care about their community / gain favourable publicity / show strong social credentials. [1] [2]

(g) (i) A premium pricing strategy sets prices above those of other competitors [1] to create a brand associated with better quality. [1] [2]

(ii) If product quality does not match the price being asked, people can associate prices with being overinflated, damaging reputation. [1] Sales may decrease as people seek value over quality. [1] [1]

1. (a) Answers in descending order down the column: (i) 339.66, (ii) 106.53, (iii) 458.13, (iv) 91.62, (v) 549.75. [5]

(b) Credit card / debit card. [1]

(c) A receipt provides the customer with a proof of purchase / payment [1] which can be used for their records / for any future dispute over the order / to activate any guarantee on faulty parts. [1] [2]

2. (a) 1-Purchase order, [1] 2-Payment, [1] 3-Statement of account. [1] [3]

(b) (i) £18.03 [1]

(ii) £941.00 [1]

(c) An SOA provides a reminder to customers of any outstanding balances / monies owed [1] which helps improve payment speed and Franco Spare's liquidity. [1]

An SOA provides an accurate record of all purchases and payments [1] which is useful to refer to when finding out about a customer. [1]

An SOA shows all of the transactions and payments between Franco Spares and a customer [1] which provides a useful reference of their track record / timeliness of payments. [1] [2]

3. (a) Staff will need to be trained to handle cash payments [1] / frequent trips to the bank will need to be made [1] to ensure that the correct change is always give out [1] which may cost time and money. [1]

Security measures such as a safe / CCTV [1] will be needed as cash will make the store a greater target for thieves. [1]
A float will be required from the bank regularly [1] to ensure that sufficient change is available in the till for transactions. [1]

Banks charge to handle cash deposits [1] which will add to an enterprise's costs. [1] [2]

(b) Service is improved [1] as more alternative choices over payment method can be offered. [1]

Speed of transactions may increase [1] because no cash / change needs to be counted out / the transaction is confirmed instantly. [1]

Transaction errors may be reduced [1] as mistakes in giving change cannot be made. [1]

Convenience is increased [1] as there is no cash to bank / process. [1]

Sales may increase [1] if customers are able to make purchases without having a wallet / the right amount of cash on them. [1] [2]

1. Two from: Heat, light and power, [1] phone bills, [1] wages. [1] [2]

2. (i) Gross profit, [1] (ii) 26 000, [1], (iii) 24 400, [1] (iv) 1600. [1] [4]

3. (a) Devon could increase selling price [1] which would increase her gross profit if she continued to sell as many units. [1]
Increase advertising and promotion [1] which would attract more customers, increasing unit sales / therefore revenue. [1] [2]

   (b) Find cheaper suppliers / negotiate discounts with existing suppliers [1] which would reduce the variable costs / costs of sale / fixed costs. [1] [2]

4. One from: Devon, the landlord, customers, suppliers. [1]

5. (a) Creditors, overdraft and tax payable are current liabilities. 4 000 + 1 300 + 3 200 = 8 500.
One mark for correctly identifying the current liabilities. One mark for a correct total. [2]

   (b) Net current assets = Current assets - current liabilities. 21 400 – 8 500 = 12 900.
Allow error carried forward from part (a). [2]

Section B5

1. (a) GPM = 61 000 ÷ 97 000 = 62.8% [2]
   (b) NPM = 18 500 ÷ 97 000 = 19.1% [2]
   (c) The enterprise has a growing NPM [1] which indicates that the enterprise is getting stronger / more efficient. [1] (ECF) [2]
   (d) Daisy Dot could increase its sales price [1] which would increase revenue, [1] Lowering prices may attract more buyers [1] which would increase overall sales revenue. [1] Reducing costs [1] would increase the profit [1], improving the margin. [2]

2. (a) Informs whether to hold off on spending [1] to ensure other costs get paid on time. [1] Provides information on whether the enterprise can afford to increase its spending / decrease its current assets [1] before getting into problems with its net asset value. [1] [2]
   (b) Perishable stock items such as cut flowers may be difficult to sell quickly before they expire [1] so leaving the inventory out of the calculation may provide a more accurate picture for the enterprise. [1] [2]
   (c) To improve Daisy Dot's liquidity, Daisy and Dorothy could sell some of the inventory. [1] to pay off some liabilities.[1] They could also look at reducing the overhead expenses. [1] which will reduce the creditors. Use longer term financing if appropriate [1] as this would move liabilities from current to long term. [1] Reduce stock/inventory in store to reduce its value [1] which would improve the liquid capital ratio. [1] Reduce any credit period to reduce the value of debtors [1] and get funds into the enterprise more quickly. [1] Chase debtors for payment [1] to increase the cash in the enterprise. [1] [2]

Section C1–3

1. (a) Two from: Purchases/materials, [1] production, [1] marketing, [1] cash. [1] [2]
   (b) A sales budget will enable Marvin to estimate how much revenue MJK Builders might make [1] which will indicate how much cash will be available for any planned expenditure. [1]
   A sales budget will inform Marvin of any likely issues before they happen [1] so measures can be put in place to avoid suffering from cash flow problems. [1] [2]

2. (a) An adverse labour budget indicates an overspend on labour compared to the budgeted figure. [1]
   (b) Marvin will need to respond by investigating his labour costs [1] to identify if there are surplus staff for the needs of the enterprise. [1] The reasons for the adverse budget will need to be discovered [1] as they could indicate a potential cash flow problem. [1] There may be an issue with the budgeted figures rather than the actual figures [1] which will inform the future budgeting for labour if the costs are all justified. [1] [2]

3. Overhead budget. The bank will want to know how much is already spent on overheads [1] to justify whether Marvin can afford the bank loan. [1]
   Labour budget. The bank will want to check how much is spent on labour [1] and will combine this with other expenditure budgets to check what their total outgoings are to see if Marvin can afford the bank loan. [1]
   Sales budget. Marvin is being asked to provide this budget to show an estimation of how many sales MJK Builders is likely to predict they will get over the year. [1] This, compared with the labour and overheads budgets will show if the enterprise is likely to remain liquid and whether a loan is a viable for Marvin / if the bank should agree to the loan. [1] [6]

4. (a) (i) 9 940 [1], (ii) (7 900) [1], (iii) 2 040 [1], (iv) (660). [1]   [4]
   (b) MJK Builders could improve its cash flow by reducing its outgoings / cost of materials. [1] In May, the outgoings are predicted to far exceed the incomings suggesting that Marvin may be overspending. If Marvin reduced staffing hours or overheads, it might help MJK Builders return to a positive cash flow. [1] Marvin could also sell off any assets the enterprise doesn't need [1] which will help Marvin cover the shortfall and enable other debts to be paid on time. [1] An investment loan from the bank [1] will help to cover the shortfall and enable further growth of the enterprise to increase sales. [1] Any debtors could be chased [1] in order to gather funds that are outstanding to cover the potential shortfall. [1] Increasing prices (in line with inflation) [1] would increase revenue and cash flow if sales did not fall as a result. [1]   [2]

Section C4–5

(a)   BEP see graph.   [4]

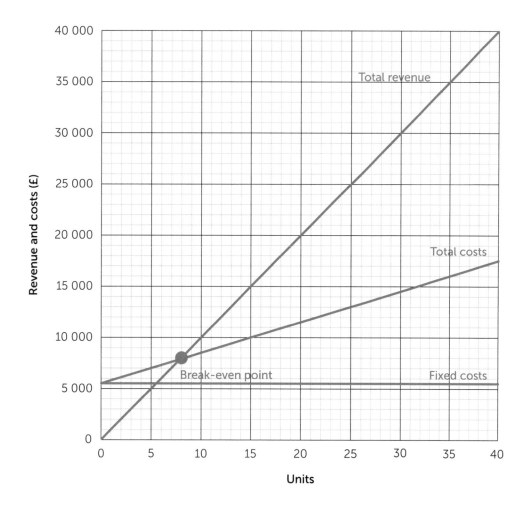

(b) (i)   BE = Fixed costs ÷ (selling price - variable costs) = 5600 / (990 − 279) = 7.87 = 8 units.
           MOS = Estimated sales - break-even point = 20 − 7.87 = 12.13 = 12 system installs.   [2]
    (ii)   It is important for Rosie and Jack to be aware of the margin of safety as they can then know how far away from being unprofitable the enterprise is. [1] They can take action if sales dip within the margin. [1]   [1]

(c)   *Intruder Scan Ltd*'s costs have increased, therefore the break-even point will shift to the right (1) and Jack will need to sell more alarm systems in order to break even. [1]   [2]

(d) It is important for *Intruder Scan Ltd* to use break even analysis so they can discover how many units the enterprise needs to sell [1] in order to break even and start making profit. [1]

Analysis enables the calculation of the margin of safety [1] which indicates the amount of leeway an enterprise has in its sales quotas before it makes a loss. [1]

It can help identify if prices are too low / costs are too high [1] so that the enterprise owners can take action. [1]

Can be a good early indicator of the viability of an enterprise [1] which can help assess the risks involved in starting up. [1]   [1]

(e) 7800 / (990 – 279) = 7800 / 711 = 10.97 = 11 installs.   [1]

(f) The additional employee would only increase the break-even point by three installations [1] and the employee should be able to install many more than that each month [1] if the sales / demand is there. Sales revenue would increase with an additional employee [1] by far more than their costs if they can install more than three systems a month. [1]   [2]

2. (a) Trade credit.   [1]

(b) This type of finance is beneficial to the enterprise because it helps them to manage their cash flow [1] by allowing them extra time to pay. [1]   [2]

(c) Responses will be credited according to the learner's demonstration of knowledge and understanding of the material, using the indicative content and level descriptors below.

The indicative content that follows is not prescriptive. Responses may cover some or all indicative content, but learners should be rewarded for other relevant responses.

Indicative content
- Rent – can leave at any time after a notice period.
- Cheaper per month
- Not responsible for upkeep of the premises
- Protection from interest rates – on a mortgage the interest rate might go up
- No money tied up in large assets
- Won't benefit if the value of the premises rises
- Mortgage – will own the property in the end
- Not exposed to large rent increases
- Property may increase in value
- Can alter the premises to your enterprises needs
- Expensive initial deposit – taking money out of the enterprise
- Would need to sell premises if the enterprise had to move location
- Interest rates can rise meaning repayments will increase
- Will need to pay for the upkeep of the property
- Any decrease in the value of the property (e.g. negative equity) will decrease long term asset value.   [6]

Long answers must be written in paragraphs. We have used bullet points here to make the answers easier to understand.
This type of question will be marked using a Levels Based Marks Scheme. See page 75 for details.

LEVELS BASED MARK SCHEME FOR EXTENDED RESPONSE QUESTIONS

Questions that require extended writing use mark bands. The whole answer will be marked together to determine which mark band it fits into and which mark should be awarded within the mark band. The first two bullet points are the same for all extended response questions. The final bullet is used for 'evaluate' questions.

Level	Descriptor
Level 3 (5–6 marks)	Demonstrates mostly accurate and thorough/detailed knowledge and understanding. Most of the points made will be relevant to the context in the question, and there will be clear links. Displays a well-developed and logical evaluation which clearly considers different aspects and competing points in detail, leading to a conclusion that is fully supported.
Level 2 (3–4 marks)	Demonstrates some accurate knowledge and understanding, with only minor gaps or omissions. Some of the points made will be relevant to the context in the question, but the link will not always be clear. Displays a partially developed evaluation which considers some different competing points, although not always in detail, leading to a conclusion which is partially supported.
Level 1 (1–2 marks)	Demonstrates few elements of knowledge and understanding. There will be major gaps or relevant knowledge left out of an answer. Few of the points made will be relevant to the context in the question. The response contains a limited evaluation which uses generic assertions leading to a conclusion that is superficial or unsupported.
0 marks	No rewardable material.

INDEX

M

managers 44
margin of safety (MOS) 60, 63
market 2, 9
  segmentation 3
marketing
  budget 52
  methods 22
  mix 12
mass market 9
materials budget 52
maturity 15
mortgage 65
multichannel marketing 19

N

net profit 41
net profit margin (NPM) 48
niche market 9

O

opening balance 55
outflows 54
overdraft 66
overheads 52
owners 44

P

payment
  methods 36
  technologies 37
payments 54
Peer to Peer lending (P2P) 65
personality characteristics 7
personal selling 18
physical distribution 17
place 17
premium pricing 16
price 16
  skimming 16
  penetration 16
pricing strategy 16
product 14
  life cycle 15
  portfolio 14
production budget 52
profit 40, 48
profitability 48
  ratios 48

profit and loss account 41
profit margin 48
promotion 18, 19
promotional budget 52
psychographics 3, 7
public relations 18
purchase order 27

Q

QR codes 18

R

race 4
radio advertising 19
receipt 32, 38, 54
record keeping 33
religion 5
remittance advice slip 32
reputation 23
retained profit 43
revenue 40, 41, 61
running costs 40

S

sales
  budget 52
  promotion 18
  receipt 32
  revenue 41, 46
segment 3
share capital 65
social
  class 7
  media 18
  responsibility 23
socio economic groups 5
solvency 48
sources of finance 64
  external 65
  internal 64
spending 8
sponsorship 23
stakeholder 44, 47, 49
start-up costs 40
statement
  of account (SOA) 33, 39
  of comprehensive income 41
  of financial position 42
suppliers 44
surplus 55

T

target market 2, 24
tax authorities 44
total assets 42
trade
  credit 66
  shows 19
traditional marketing 12
trust 23
turnover 40

U

unethical practice 23
usage rate 8
USP (Unique Selling Point) 14

V

variable costs 61
variance 53
VAT 27

W

working capital 42

NOTES, DOODLES AND EXAM DATES

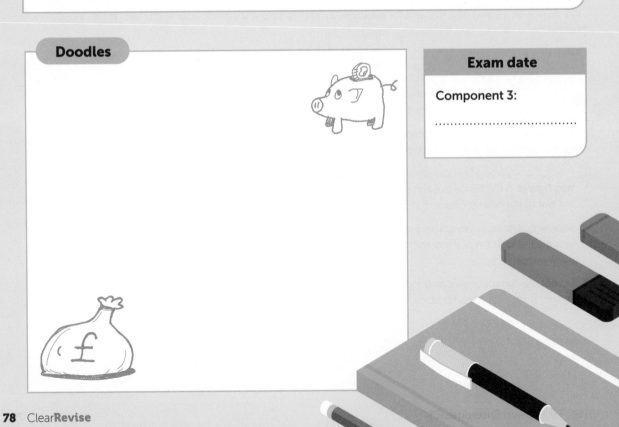

Doodles

Exam date

Component 3:

....

EXAMINATION TIPS

With your examination practice, use a boundary approximation using the following table. Be aware that boundaries are usually a few percentage points either side of this.

Grade	L1 Pass	L1 Merit	L1 Distinction	L2 Pass	L2 Merit	L2 Distinction
Boundary	30%	40%	50%	60%	70%	80%

1. Be prepared with a black pen, a calculator, and a ruler.

2. Read the scenario to ensure that your answers are in context. Circle, underline or highlight key parts to help you to answer correctly. Re-visit the scenario several times during the examination and re-familiarise yourself with it.

3. Read each question carefully. You cannot get marks for giving an answer to a question you think is appearing rather than the actual question. Avoid simply rewriting the question or repeating examples that are already given in the question.

4. Read the question and its stem thoroughly to ensure your answer is focused correctly e.g., an advantage to the enterprise, or an advantage to the customer.

5. *Give* questions require you to recall a short piece of key information. No explanation is required. There will be one mark for each point you make.

6. Where two examples are asked for, avoid giving two similar examples. For example, if you are asked to give two types of budgets, avoid giving both marketing and promotion, or purchases and materials as these terms mean the same thing. Labour and overheads would be a better answer as they are different examples of budgets.

7. Remember that *explain* questions have two marks. You need to make a point for the first mark, and then expand this point with a linked development for the second mark. To help you develop your responses, aim to include connective words such as 'because' or 'so'.

8. Avoid undeveloped answers such as 'quick', 'simple', 'fast' and 'easy'. These cannot be awarded marks.

9. There are two long answer questions on each paper. These are each awarded 6 marks and use the command verbs *discuss* and *evaluate*. Remember that the answers to these questions need both advantages **and** disadvantages, and an '*evaluate*' question also needs a conclusion.

10. Be sure to learn the formulae needed to calculate revenue, gross profit, net profit (profit for the year), working capital (net current assets), break-even and margin of safety as they are **not** given in the examination.

11. Practice completing financial documents and statements. Those documents that show pence always require **two figures** in the pence column e.g. £5.00, £17.99 or £103.05. Figures may be rounded up to the nearest penny, but **not** to the nearest pound.

12. Answer questions in the spaces provided. If this is not possible, for instance, you have deleted a wrong answer, indicate the location of the corrected answer on the paper (e.g. '*see next page*' or '*my answer is on the last blank page*').

13. Do not use the space allocated for answers to write plans for your answers, and do not add extra pages to your answer book with plans/scribbles/items that will not be marked.

Good luck!

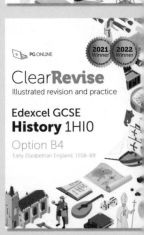